Rendering Divine Names on Coins

Rendering Divine Names on Coins

Images from Antiquity to Modern Times

David Bentley
AND
Brad Yonaka

FOREWORD BY
Jonas Mark Hayes

WIPF & STOCK · Eugene, Oregon

RENDERING DIVINE NAMES ON COINS
Images from Antiquity to Modern Times

Copyright © 2019 David Bentley and Brad Yonaka. All rights reserved. Except for brief quotations in critical publications or reviews, no part of this book may be reproduced in any manner without prior written permission from the publisher. Write: Permissions, Wipf and Stock Publishers, 199 W. 8th Ave., Suite 3, Eugene, OR 97401.

Wipf & Stock
An Imprint of Wipf and Stock Publishers
199 W. 8th Ave., Suite 3
Eugene, OR 97401

www.wipfandstock.com

PAPERBACK ISBN: 978-1-5326-7069-5
HARDCOVER ISBN: 978-1-5326-7070-1
EBOOK ISBN: 978-1-5326-7071-8

Scripture quotations are from Revised Standard Version of the Bible, copyright 1946, 1952, and 1971 National Council of the Churches of Christ in the United States of America. Used by permission. All rights reserved worldwide.

Manufactured in the U.S.A.   04/10/20

"A man of flesh and blood produces many coins from the same die. They are all identical. But the King of Kings (that is God) stamps out all men in the die of Adam the first man. Yet not one man is identical with his fellow man."

—*The Talmud*

Contents

Foreword by Jonas Mark Hayes | vii
Preface and Acknowledgments | ix
Abbreviations of Books of the Bible | xiii
Photo and Figure Permissions | xiv

Chapter 1: Monarchs' Lesser Gods—*Pharaoh Akhenaton and Indian Aśoka* | 1
Chapter 2: Hebrew Divine Names—*Laws and Prophets* | 12
Chapter 3: Gospels of Jesus—*Kerygma of the Incarnation and Kingdom of God* | 26
Chapter 4: Greet the New Smiths—*Paul, Priscilla, Aquila: Tabernacle-makers, Not Tentmakers* | 41
Chapter 5: Gnosticism—*Abracadabra and Nag Hammadi Texts* | 57
Chapter 6: Saints of the Orthodox East—*Icons and Iconoclasts* | 67
Chapter 7: Zoroaster and Ahuramazada—*This Zarathustra Spoke* | 80
Chapter 8: Muhammad, Prophet of Allah—*The Qur'an Speaks Arabic* | 87
Chapter 9: Abbasid Rise and Fall—*Political Drifts, Spiritual Uplifts* | 98
Chapter 10: Manichaeism—*Dualism along the Silk Road* | 107
Chapter 11: Turks, Crusader, Mongols—*Outlanders Besiege Arab Islam* | 114
Chapter 12: Antiquity in US Coins—*"In God We Trust"* | 124

Appendix A | 133
Appendix B | 135
Bibliography | 137
Index | 141

Foreword

THE BOOK OF GENESIS contains a pair of obscure verses that in truth hold the root of today's headlines. In these two verses, we can find the pathos of 4,000 years of Jewish, Muslim, and Christian history. In these two verses, we find the source of 2.4 billion Christians, 1.8 billion Muslims, and 14 million Jews within the family of Abraham:

> Abraham breathed his last and died in a good old age, an old man and full of years, and was gathered to his people. Isaac and Ishmael his sons buried him in the cave of Machpelah. (Gen 25:8–9 RSV)

That is utterly shocking that Isaac and Ishmael stood side by side at their father's graveside. Isaac and Ishmael hated each other, seeing each other as rivals since before they were even born. Abraham did in death what he could never do in life: he brought his two sons together.

Scripture does not hide the unseemly side of our faith ancestors. Scripture lays bare the corrosive relationships in our family history. God's word cuts away all false piety and exposes the pus underneath.

Picture the scene. There at the graveside, Ishmael and Isaac—the heads of two opposing nations—stand side by side. It was not a Hallmark moment or the makings of a Lifetime movie. They didn't hug. They didn't say to each other, "Let's go have some coffee and talk. I have some apologizing to do." They did not shake hands. They stood side by side. That is all.

How might Ishmael and Isaac standing side by side in Genesis 25 help us to rethink, change, or encourage the way we interact with others?

David Bentley and Brad Yonaka, in their work *Rendering Divine Names on Coins,* offer a timely interfaith discussion, encouraging all people to learn more of the divine, our higher power, whom we call upon with many different names. Through their extensive and thoughtful research, Bentley and Yonaka thoroughly explore ancient and modern coins from a variety of contexts as a way for readers not only to learn about our various societies and cultures, but also to find clues about God.

In this timely work, Bentley and Yonaka introduce a fresh and thought-provoking claim of St. Paul and other early Christians as "tablernacle-makers" (silversmiths) instead of "tentmakers," as most commonly thought. Bentley's innovative biblical scholarship paired with Yonaka's metallurgic expertise reveal how openly St. Paul and his companions engaged a topic that many find uncomfortable—financial stewardship—as a necessary and meaningful way to do God's work. Such a perspective prods congregations and faith-based leaders today to consider how God calls us to "love God with all of our possessions," as the Torah says, and how our stewardship of our body, as well as our resources, offers a lens into our faith.

Each coin bears an image or a likeness. So, too, do we, as a diverse people who come from the ancestry from Ishmael and Isaac, bear the likeness of our Creator, which we are called to render or give back to God. As you read, in the unity and peace in the sisterhood and brotherhood of our one worldwide human family, may we seek to render or give back that which belongs to God, remembering that common bloodline rooted in Isaac and Ishmael. When we harken back to their story, we remember: we are kin who share a promise that the God whom we call upon with many different names will never leave nor forsake us.

Rev. Jonas Mark Hayes
Grace First Presbyterian Church
Long Beach, California

Preface and Acknowledgments

RENDERING DIVINE NAMES ON *Coins* presents our attempts to find clues about God and gods on ancient and modern coins. Our Bentley-Yonaka team met for the first time five years ago in a local coin collector club where we discovered a mutual devotion to coins and the fact that we previously lived in separate countries of the Middle East. Brad keeps expanding his interest and has published three books about Spanish Colonial coins. David first published *The 99 Beautiful Names of God for all the People of the Book* in 1999, and followed with three other books. Each publication, along with this current writing, emphasizes the names of God in words calling for a deeper understanding of Muslims who represent one-fourth of the world's population. Brad's professional education and career relates directly to metallurgy, which guides his thinking about a coin's metallic constituents of gold, silver, and lesser-valued metals. His analysis of a coin's weight and its mintage was a significant contribution to the creation of this book. Our interpretation of the coins' scripts have been a common challenge as we scanned over 3,500 years of mintage coins.

In searching for coins with the divine names, we turned to the Scriptures—both Hebrew and Greek—the Holy Qur'an, and commentaries on Zoroastrianism and Manichaeism. The book is neither an interfaith work nor an apologia for a specific branch of the Abrahamic traditions. Our passionate hope is to bolster peaceful contact among Jewish, Christian, and Islamic pastoral and spiritual leaders and their lay communities. These interactions have not always been cordial, as evidenced by our world's long history of rivalries and bloody conflicts.

The figures on the following pages will reveal that the rarest of all the earth's elements—gold—has enabled kings to wage war and pay bribes for truces and ransoms. On the lower end of this social scale, the tiny bronze and copper coins are worn smooth by the fingers of peasant food producers and widows, as in the gospel narrative of the widow's mite. Between these two coins and their metals is the silver found in the money bags of middlemen, primarily of priests, military and civil servants, local bazzaris, and other international traders such as Marco Polo.

Our title focuses on the spoken words of Jesus when Jewish authorities asked him about paying taxes to Caesar. A Roman coin with Tiberius's image suddenly appears out of the bag of one the tax lawyers stationed inside the Jerusalem Temple. The Tiberius silver denarius was a suitable coin for the half-shekel Temple tax. However, Jesus' statement astonishes the orthodox religious Pharisees and the politically savvy Herodians: "Render therefore to Caesar the things that are Caesar's and to God, the things that are God's." For believers and nonbelievers alike, this statement from Matthew 22:21 commands honor to God and the State under a purloined headline for tax reform. All generations found the dual renderings to God and to Caesar a bewildering command, as this book will show.

Another New Testament portion asks the reader to heed the apostle of the gentiles, Paul's appeal to the Roman non-Jewish believers in Jesus about honoring and respecting the original children of Abraham. Paul develops this plea based on the Grecian coin with a bust of Athena. The book's foremost premise is that Paul and Aquila and Priscilla earned a living that paid for their evangelistic efforts in the minting of coins and by marketing mini-tabernacles as pieces of jewelry.

A roster of renowned and obscure names represents the book's binary diversity: Sts. John of Damascus and the enigmatic Dionysius the Pseudo-Areopagite, Genghis Khan and St. Francis of Assi, Moses of the book of Genesis and Moses of the Qur'an. Not all of these prime-time characters got profiled on coins, but each prayed to God with variant names.

We ask our readers for their indulgence in the use of many words which do not conform to common English spelling. The solution is somewhat simplified by our use of the Latin alphabet with a liberal amount of italicization when we transliterated Hebrew, Greek, Aramaic, and Arabic texts. Also all references to the Muslim calendar's AH year (*anno hajj*), are mentioned in the immediate contexts of the BC and AD (*anno domino*) dates.

We would like to thank Stephen Album and Dudley Woodberry for their endorsements early in our writing project. Wayne Sayles's offers to assist have been accepted over several personal contacts that go back many years. Jerry Kleeb deserves our praise for his valuable suggestions

PREFACE AND ACKNOWLEDGMENTS

on coins whenever we met at local coin clubs. Our acknowledgments are extended to Pastor Jonas Mark Hayes for his thoughtful and encouraging word in the Foreword. He stands in his pulpit as do other church, synagogue, and mosque preachers who often serve their congregations in trying economic conditions. My son, Jon Bentley, worked with Brad in sketching many of the figures that appear on the following pages. Our thanks go out to the staff of Wipf and Stock, and our editor Matt Wimer, for his thoughtful, encouraging words.

Finally, we thank our wives, Isabel and Janet, who willingly exceeded all expectations to lovingly serve us during the last five years. We'll project our thanks to our adult and tender-aged children and all succeeding grandchildren by wishing and praying God's peace for all their futures.

David Bentley and Brad Yonaka

Long Beach, CA, February, 2019

Abbreviations

Books of the Bible arranged alphabetically with New Testament indicated by *italics*. Revised Standard Version of Bible (RSV) is used exclusively.

Acts	*Acts*	John	*John*
Amos	Amos	1 Kings	1 Kgs
1 Chronicles	1 Chr	2 Kings	2 Kgs
2 Chronicles	2 Chr	Leviticus	Lev
1 Corinthians	*1 Cor*	Luke	*Luke*
2 Corinthians	*2 Cor*	Mark	*Mark*
Esther	Esth	Mathew	*Matt*
Daniel	Dan	Numbers	Num
Deuteronomy	Deut	Philippians	*Phil*
Exodus	Exod	Proverbs	Prov
Galatians	*Gal*	Psalms	Ps
Genesis	Gen	Romans	*Rom*
Hebrews	*Heb*	2 Samuel	2 Sam
Isaiah	Isa	1 Timothy	*1 Tim*
James	*Jas*	2 Timothy	*2 Tim*

Photo and Figure Permissions

Figures 01, 02, 03, 11, 19, 28, 32, 39, 55, 64, 75, 80, and 89 are sketches by author Brad Yonaka. Figures 04, 12, 16, 31, 41, 44, 46, 51, 62, and 70 courtesy Wikimedia Commons. Figure 05 courtesy Chris Nauton. Figures 06, 09, 30, 38, 50, 53, 54, 58, 59, 72, 73, 85, 88, 90 (right), 91 (right), 92 (right), 93 (right), 94 (right), and 96 (all coins) are photos by author Brad Yonaka. Figures 07, 08, and 47 courtesy *Wildwinds.com*. Figure 10 courtesy A. H. Baldwin & Sons Ltd. Figures 13 and 24 are sketches by Jon Bentley. Figures 14, cover image, and 34 courtesy Ira and Larry Goldberg. Figures 15, 63, and 71 reproduced by kind permission of Spink and Son Ltd, London. Figures 17, 78, and 92 (left) courtesy Heritage Auctions. Figures 18, 26, 27, 29, 35, 37, 52, 60, 66–68, 74, 76, 77, 79, 81, 82, 83 (left), 87, and 91 (left) courtesy *zeno.ru* coin website. Figure 20 courtesy Athena Numismatics Ltd. Figure 21 reproduced courtesy Web Gallery of Art. Figures 22, 25, 36, 40, and 48 courtesy Classical Numismatic Group, Inc., cng@cngcoins.com. Figure 23 courtesy Numismatica Ars Classica NAC AG, Auction 94, lot 77. Figure 33 courtesy of Praefectus Coins. Figure 42 courtesy Wayne G. Sayles. Figure 43 courtesy Aaron Berk. Figure 45 courtesy *Wildwinds.com*, ex-Goldberg auction 2008. Figure 49 courtesy David Lowe. Figure 56 courtesy image from *clipart.com*. Figure 57 courtesy Steve Battelle. Figure 61 courtesy Sonia Halliday Photo Library. Figure 65 courtesy of Michael Bezayiff. Figure 69 courtesy Steve Album, fixed price list #154033. Figure 83 (left) courtesy Steve Album, Auction 25, lot 2203. Figure 84 courtesy Morton & Eden Auction 48, April 2011, lot 67. Figure 86 courtesy Steve Album, Auction 25, lot 651. Figure 90 (left) courtesy © Bruun Rasmussen Auctioneers. Figure 93 (left) courtesy Bertolami Fine Arts. Figure 94 (left) reprinted with permission by David Hendin © 2005. Figure 95 courtesy Steve Album, Auction 21, lot 1812. Figure 97 courtesy Steve Album, Auction 24, lot 488.

1

Monarchs' Lesser Gods

Pharaoh Akhenaten and Indian Aśoka

AN EGYPTIAN PHARAOH OF the fourteenth century BC and an Indian monarch of the second century BC provide modern models for improvised tweets and gossipy social sound bites. The pharaoh and the Indian Aśoka upended their respective nations' historical courses to pursue innovative political tactics that would not be reinvigorated until the present day. Pharaoh Akhenaten's fascination with monotheism and Aśoka's experimentation with secularism were both on trial during their reigns, leaving many religious and political questions unanswered that puzzle contemporary scholars and laypersons today. The most valid of archaeological markers are coins, but they had not yet been invented in Akhenaten's reign, a time when the tombs of pharaohs filled the Egyptian landscape. Non-Greek coins in the Aśoka regime were silver, angular, and locally minted. As such, Aśoka's heraldry symbols in modern India are lions mounted on towers, rather than any similar symbolism on the coins of his time.

The father of Amenhotep IV, Amenhotep III, performed the expected actions of a dominant pharaoh that secured him a place among the eternal-past Egyptians.

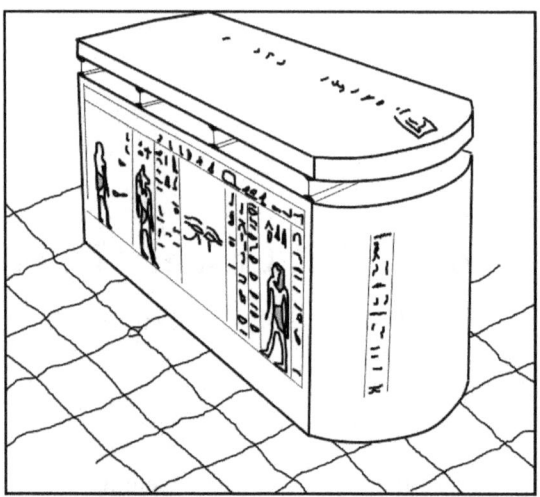

Fig. 01—Amenhotep III Sarcophagus

Egypt's borders extended from Anatolia in the north to the Nubian gold mines in the south. These rich sources of royal wealth were deftly exploited by pharaohs throughout the New Kingdom period, and Amenhotep III was no exception. To enemies and allies alike, his diplomatic dispatches offered or refused requests for gold and his daughters in marriage as part of Pharaoh Amenhotep's communication system connecting his expanding empire. Tablets uncovered from the last years of Amenhotep III's life show exchanges of letters with vassal kings of Western Asia from Gaza through Canaan, Syria, and Babylon. A second form of the pharaoh's communication with his empire was the distribution of scarabs throughout the region and islands of the Eastern Mediterranean Sea.[1] These oversized commemorative scarabs served as empire sound bites and a gazette of the often mundane undertakings of the pharaoh, including news of his hunting expeditions and four marriages. Both the scarabs and the Amarna letters were written in Babylonian cuneiform script.

---

1. O'Connor, *Amenhotep III*, 232.

Fig. 02—Scarab Hieroglyphic Script

A third method of communication involves the *Hymn to Aton* which was discovered in an Amarna tomb excavated in 1891. The hymn, dedicated to Aton, or Aten, the Sun-disc god, was written in Egyptian hieroglyphics and contains some verses from Amenhotep III's reign (pre-1390 BC). Biblical scholar James Pritchard compares some Egyptian proverbs in the *Hymn to Aton*[2] with Hebrew and Greek Scriptures including this one from Proverbs 22:24-25:

> Make no friendship with a man given to anger, nor go with a wrathful man, lest you learn his ways and entangle yourself in a snare.[3]

> Aton Hymn xi: Preserve thy tongue from answering thy superior,/ And guard thyself against reviling him./Do not make him cast his speech to lasso thee.[4]

The Hebrew scholar Edgar J. Young writes that Proverbs 22 and 23 reveal close parallels with the Hymn of Aton: "Be not one of those who give pledges,/who become surety for debts./If you have nothing with which to pay,/why should your bed be taken from under you?"[5] Young claims that

---

2. Pritchard, *Ancient Near East*, 240.
3. Prov 22:24–25 RSV.
4. Pritchard, *Ancient Near East*, xi.
5. Young, *Introduction to the Old Testament*, 331. See also Prov 22:27 RSV.

the Proverbs material was written prior to the Aton Hymn during Amenhotep III's reign. He translates two citations from the Aton Hymn:

> If thou findest a large debt against a poor man,/make it into three parts,/Forgive two, and let one stand./Thou wilt find it like the ways of life;/Thou will lie down and sleep (soundly).[6] Control your temper, save your life./Do not steer your life with your tongue alone./Make your tongue the rudder of your boat./But make Amon-Ra its pilot.[7]

The Book of James offers:

> Look at the ships also; though they are so great and are driven by strong winds, they are guided by a very small rudder. . . So the tongue is a little member and boasts of great things. . .[8]

The Aton Hymn calls for just weights.

> Do not lean on the scales nor falsify weights/Nor damage the fractions of a measure./Do not wish for a (common) measure.[9]

And Proverbs affirms:

> A just balance and scales are the Lord's; all the weights in the bag are his work.[10] Diverse weights are an abomination to the Lord, and false scales are not good.[11]

Amenhotep IV changed his name to Akhenaten after the god, Aten, when he moved his capital from Thebes to the new Amarna site, about 100 miles south of Cairo. During his early years of an eighteen-year reign, a cartouche revealed his attachment to the god Aten.

---

6. Pritchard, *Ancient Near East*, xv.
7. Pritchard, *Ancient Near East*, 280.
8. Jas 3:4–5 RSV.
9. Pritchard, *Ancient Near East*, xvii.
10. Prov 16:11 RSV.
11. Prov 20:23 RSV.

MONARCHS' LESSER GODS

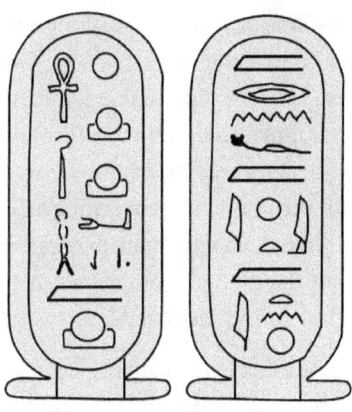

Fig. 03—Cartouche Akhenaten

Pharaoh Akhenaten never rejected his own god-king divine names when he maneuvered to divert attention away from the priests who resisted the reforms of the old religious order. The new pharaoh did little to propagate his monotheistic tendencies in letters that his father would regularly send to neighboring countries. An indication of Akhenaten's revolutionary theology were the monuments and tombs with pillars and statues often portraying the pharaoh and his family facing inward rather than outward beyond the walls. A daily full sun's rays confirmed the pharaoh's deification.

Fig. 04—Akhenaten Family under Sun God

Existing representations of Akhenaten, along with other circumstantial evidence, suggests this king, along with his son Tutankhamun (popularly named King Tut), suffered from a disease that left them physically deformed. Akhenaten's wife, Nefertiti, played an important role as a beloved queen and when she mysteriously disappeared from the scene, Akhenaten's world fell apart. He lost touch with the realities of governing an empire and guiding the dynamics of the new faith in Aten which the priests were more capable of opposing once in control of the Nubian gold mines in Upper Egypt. Historian John Bright appraises the monotheism of Aten:

> [W]e must record the fact that less than a century before Moses a religion of monotheistic character had emerged in Egypt. Whether it was truly that has caused debate; the pharaoh was himself regarded as god. . . Yet Aten was hailed as the sole god, creator of all things, beside (or like) whom is no other.[12]

Pharaoh Tutankhamun's short reign of about ten years did not produce an heir. He inherited the Aten theology from his father, but the lack of a bloodline precluded continuance of the cult. In any event, possibly under pressure from his advisors, he reversed many of his father's religious influences back to earlier traditions. His body was hastily buried and fortunately forgotten until the twentieth century. The golden funeral mask and sarcophagi amaze visitors to the Cairo Museum. A hieroglyphic reminder of the Sun God, Aten, is observable on his throne.

---

12. Bright, *History of Israel*, 100.

Fig. 05—Tutankhamun's Throne

When the Amarna artifacts were destroyed, as was the city; monotheism would be on hold for a century. The dynasty of Egypt's New Age comes to an inelegant end with the eradication of a monotheistic concept that bore a slight resemblance to the Hebrew faith.

Over a millennium after Akhenaten, another emperor adopted a religious name, "Beloved of the Gods," and proceeded carefully to proclaim his personal adaptations of Buddhism. And, while Akhenaten withdrew from the public eye and built private monuments, Aśoka followed his model by posting his *Dhamma*, not in scrolls of proverbs, but more akin to the scattering of the newsy scarabs by mounting lions on a pillar that today are engraved on rupees circulating throughout the Republic of India.

Fig. 06—Aśokan Modern Pillar Coin

The emperor of all India began his reign at the closing of the Mauryas Dynasty. This dynasty endured in the midst of constant wars in the northren frontier town of Taxila, where in 327 BC Alexander the Great met the Mauryas kingdom's predecessors' armed elephants that led to Alexander's defeat and his abandonment of further Asian ventures. Aśoka's biographer, Romila Thapar, thoroughly reports on his luminary life, as well as his dark side when he had six of his half-brothers put to death.[13]

Four years into his reign in 248 BC, he became a Buddhist after visiting the garden where Buddha was born; a pillar with an inscription marks this location in Lumbini.[14] Hindi Brahmans were loyal to the Maurya throne. When he died in 232 BC, he left behind half a mango, a testament to his abandonment of material things. His *Dhamma*, as enshrined on The Thirteenth Major Rock Edict, is the longest of Aśoka's proclamations that declared his personal piety directed at the Kalinga Province on the Bay of Bengal's east coast of India. This edict was also found in Kandahar, in present-day Afghanistan. The very name of this city comes from Alexander, who established this outpost during his campaign about seventy years before these two Greek and Aramaic edicts would be posted on rocks. Contemporary kings of Aśoka who supposedly shared the Indian emperor's optimistic Dhamma are identified on these edicts. Two of Alexander the Great's successors—an Antiochus and a Ptolemy—are listed on the rocks' edicts. These have been identified as Greek Kings Antiochus II and Ptolemy II and date the rock edicts at 256–57 BC.[15] Antiochus' inheritance

---

13. Thapar, *Aśoka and the Decline*, 32.
14. Thapar, *Aśoka and the Decline*, 63.
15. Thapar, *Aśoka and the Decline*, 51.

was the Seleucid territory bordering the Indian Empire, while the Ptolemies were based primarily in Egypt and its capital, Alexandria. These two kings were constantly at war with each other over the large Syrian territory between them. The two coins do not reveal any signs of peace with each other or with Aśoka's overtures for peace based on Buddhism. Antiochus II and Ptolemy II are portrayed as Greek gods on the obverse, or face, of their coins. It is significant that these two kings chose such blatant self-deification by honoring themselves in this way, relegating the depictions of the gods to the reverse side. Antiochus II's seated nude god and Ptolemy II's god Melqarth symbolized Greek dominance that was countered by Aśoka's rough-edged coins and self-deprecating decrees.

Fig. 07—King Antiochus II Coin

Fig. 08—Ptolemy II Coin

The emperor's royal name, "Beloved of the Gods," is inscribed several times on the Thirteenth Rock and discloses his Dhamma, which was not part of any formal Buddhist practice but a way of life that Aśoka extracted from his own experience. He describes a faith that moved away from warfare along with personal regrets when he begs forgiveness for the murder of his half-brothers, his brutal conquest of Kalinga, and treatment of forest tribals (the untouchables), who were admonished to remain calm and self-controlled. Here he refers to his eternal triumphs:

> What is obtained by this victory everywhere and everywhere victory is pleasant. This pleasure has been obtained through victory by Dhamma, yet it is but a slight pleasure for the Beloved of the Gods only looks upon that as important in its results which pertains to the next world.[16]

The silver coins here show punch-marks that Thapar identifies.

Fig. 09—Aśokan Punch-mark Coins

The coin on the left has in its upper left at 9 o'clock a horned figure, a downward U, as a symbol for 'horns of divinity.'[17] At five o'clock is a dot within a circle that is interpreted as symbol for warfare.[18] This wheel is central to Indian flag emblems. On the coin on the right, the single punch-mark represents a tree.[19] Aśoka's and Akhenaten's attempts to unify their nations involved momentous changes in religious attitudes. With his idiosyncrasies and wide domestic rejection, the Egyptian pharaoh had a very short time to experiment with monotheism. Aśoka's leadership and Buddhist belief as expressed in Dhamma assured stability while he was on the throne, but

16. Thapar, *Aśoka and the Decline*, 384.
17. Thapar, *Aśoka and the Decline*, 369.
18. Thapar, *Aśoka and the Decline*, 384.
19. Thapar, *Aśoka and the Decline*, 366–67.

failed to secure a lasting peace for his people. On the international scenes, both nations faced opportunistic neighbors who took advantage of the perceived weaknesses of Egypt and India. Later sovereign nations applied the messages of their kings and caliphs on coins that could pass through sealed borders, spreading commerce, with some buried in dirt to later enrich those who unearthed them. Coins continue to act as both contemporary and eternal promotional trinkets for their sovereign rulers, their prevailing gods, and even their lowly minters.

2

Hebrew Divine Names

Laws and Prophets

MOSES IS THE CREDITED author of the first five books of the Hebrew Bible, known as the Torah or Mosaic Law. According to Jewish mystical author Neil Asher Silberman, the 613 commandments and obligations of the Law are associated with the number of Adam's body parts.[1] Among this number of laws are the universally recognized Ten Commandments (Exod 20:1–17) and the very specific commandment of separating meat and dairy foods. After this detail of setting up kosher kitchens, Moses came down from Mt. Sinai with an added commandment:

> ". . . You shall not boil a kid in its mother's milk." And the LORD said to Moses, "Write these words; in accordance with these words I have made a covenant with you and with Israel."[2]

During Moses' forty days on the mountain, the Lord had previously commanded:

> "When you take the census of the people of Israel, then each shall give a ransom for himself to the LORD when you number them, that there be no plague among them when you number them. Each who is numbered in the census shall give this: half a shekel according to the shekel of the sanctuary (the shekel is twenty gerahs), half a shekel as an offering to the LORD.[3]

This census is further described as ransom, a modern insurance policy that also spelled out identical payments by the rich and the poor.

---

1. Silberman, *Heavenly Powers*, 185.
2. Exod 34:26–27 RSV.
3. Exod 30:12–13 RSV.

The shekels were minted in the Canaanite port of Tyre and, since the silver content was very stable, this coin became fully certified for Temple payment. The gerah was a bronze copy of the Greek goddess Athena coin with an olive wreath on her head. Both the shekel and the gerah were not to be minted for hundreds of years after lawgiver Moses' death.

Fig. 10—Gerah, a Jewish Coin Imitative of a Greek Type

The silver and the bronze coins introduced at this time in the Bible are patently anachronisms that reveal the editing of older documents to fit some current issues. Biblical scholars are constantly searching for indications of reediting of the names of God in the books of Moses. Elohim is the name in Genesis 1, but LORD God is the name in chapters 2 and 3. This change of names undergirds the hypothesis regarding alterations and additions to the original Elohim texts by adding the Yahweh name. Those who did the editing had to have the skills, as well as authority, to do this, which means this could only have come about from the priestly class. The function of the copyist-priest was to assure that Yahweh's name was added to the older Elohim documents. The rewriting, like the countermarks on Aśokan, Persian, and Greek coins, was an acceptable practice. Marked-up coins were counted as part of the original—neither illegal, nor an imitation. For centuries, coin or text recertification guaranteed the item was genuine and not a counterfeit nor plagiarism, but a way of honoring the first editions and any secondary editions of a coin.

Before examining the name Lord, the *Am who I Am (YWHH)*, as revealed to Moses, we will glance back at another use of the name in Genesis 12:1 and 2 when the Lord spoke to Abram, later Abraham, in the polytheistic Haran district of Mesopotamia.

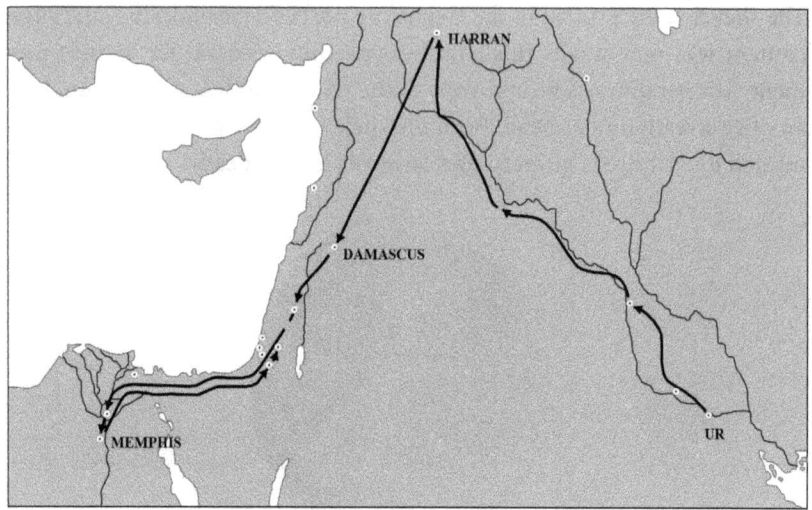

Fig. 11—Abraham's Journey from Ur to Bethel

> Now the LORD said to Abram, "Go from your country and your kindred and your father's house to the land that I will show you. And I will make of you a great nation; and I will bless you, and make your name great..."[4]

Sarai (later Sarah) and her husband, Abram, agree on the dismissal of Sarai's maidservant, Hagar, the Egyptian (16:1, 5). An angel appears to Hagar near a spring in the desert shortly after Ishmael, her son by Abraham, is born (16:7, 16). Later, Sarah's son, Isaac, is the second son, but the one intended to be sacrificed by his father before the Lord's angel intervenes to renew the covenant with Abraham (22:11–18). In a strictly nonceremonious, commercial deal, Abraham purchases for 400 silver shekels a burial place that survives in Hebron for close to three millennia (see Appendix B). The descendants of the Abrahamic faith who pray at this tomb are confronted by the Islamic version, an Arabic recertification of older accounts, by which Hagar replaces Sarah and Ishmael replaces Isaac as Abraham's first-born son.

Exodus, the second of the five books of Moses, delineates the covenants introduced in the book of Genesis. YHWH is the Creator-Originator of the covenants and the Enforcer-Enabler of the terms by which his servant-patriarchs—namely Abraham, Isaac, and Jacob—will be held accountable.

4. Gen 12:1–2 RSV.

Sinai, renamed Mt. Horeb, becomes the sacred mount where Moses and the new people of God will assume a party-of-the-second-part, suzerain relationship. After running away from treacherous conditions for himself and his fellow Hebrews enslaved in Egypt, Moses hears the angel of the Lord at the burning bush. With reservations, Moses will return to Egypt, but not before the encounter with Elohim who introduces a new name, YHWH, *I am who I am*. (Gen 3:4). After the ten plagues which YHWH inflicts on Egypt, including the death of Pharaoh's first-born son and the loss of his army in the Red Sea, Moses leads his people into the Sinai wilderness where God reveals himself again. The mountain erupts with thunder, fire, and smoke as God speaks the *Decalogue*, Ten Words, opening with, "I am the LORD your God, who brought you out of the land of Egypt. . ."[5] Moses smashes the tablets after seeing the golden calf which was constructed during his lingering on the mountain.

Fig. 12—Idol of the Golden Calf

5. Exod 20:2 RSV.

Jewelry, golden earrings, and other amulets brought out of Egypt with images of pharaonic gods, are melted down to create the idol that Moses' brother Aaron was shamelessly supervising (Exod 32:1–6). In a second effort to join the sons of Israel to the covenant, Moses receives instructions about another authenticating symbol of the Lord's presence with the construction of the temporary and portable tabernacle. Hovering over this huge tent of many animal skins was a cloud by day and a fire by night. (Exod 40:34–38).

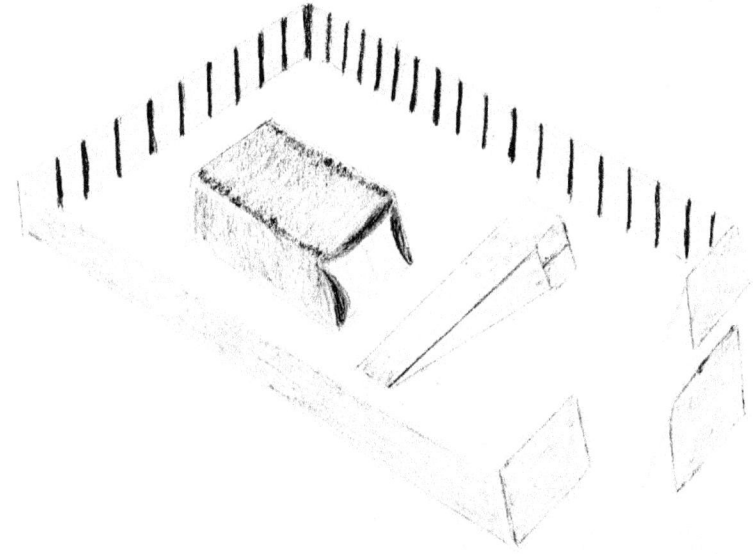

Fig. 13—Tabernacle in Wilderness

The next three books of Moses—Leviticus, Numbers, and Deuteronomy—spell out the conditions of the covenant between the Lord and the children of Israel. Sacred rituals and Sabbath ordinances blend with the civil codes which are renewed when the former Hebrew slaves in Egypt take possession of the promised land. Deuteronomy was edited later than the other books of Moses, and its message describes high regard for the priests, the custodians of the Temple funds. Moses' final words reveal the Lord's concerns for the poor, the stranger in the land, the widows and orphans (Deut 34), as well as the integrity of weights and measures. A general command to the people is repeated later to the priests.

Fig. 14—Shekels and Just Weights

> You shall not have in your bag two kinds of weights, a large and a small. You shall not have in your house two kinds of measures, a large and a small. A full and just weight you shall have . . . that your days may be prolonged in the land which the LORD your God gives you.[6]

The priests in the book of Leviticus are not only charged to love the stranger, but also to set the scales for just measurements: "You shall have just balances, just weights, a just ephah and a just hin: I am the LORD your God, who brought you out of the land of Egypt."[7] Within a few generations, after the defeat of the Israelites and the capture of the Ark of the Covenant, a prophetess proclaims that Israel's former glory days have passed (1 Sam 4:21). The word "glory" arises from an abstract idea signifying honor and reverence, but etymologically it means "heavy" and is associated with the word "shekel," meaning a thing weighed. By the eighth century BC, two writing prophets—Amos and Hosea—are assailing the ill-gotten gains of the people of Judah and Israel. Amos mocks the arrogance of the rich by proclaiming:

> Hear this, you who trample upon the needy/and bring the poor of the land to an end,/saying, "When will the new moon be over,/ that we may sell grain? And the sabbath, that we may offer wheat for sale,/That we make the ephah small and the shekel great,. . ./ that we may buy the poor for silver/and the needy for a pair of sandals". . .[8]

6. Deut 25:13–14 RSV.
7. Lev 19:36 RSV.
8. Amos 8:4–6 RSV.

David, Israel's second king, occupies the center of regal authority during his, his sons', and his grandsons' reigns, the kings of Judah, for nearly five centuries. His bloodlines run through Mary and Joseph, promising the Messiah, the Anointed, *Christos*. David's checkered life informs the Psalms' readers about his multi-personage, beginning as a boy shepherd (chapter 23), a rebel (54), a forgiven murderer (51), and a king (61). David's prayer (Ps 17:8) asks the LORD to keep him as the apple of his eye, apparently recertifying the final words of Moses in which Jacob is the pupil/apple of God's eye (Deut 32:10). Author and Holy Land pilgrim Bruce Feiler makes a compelling assessment while searching for the tomb of David in Jerusalem's Old City. Feiler notices a synagogue built by first-century Christians where archaeologists have uncovered levels of Crusader, Byzantine, and Roman churches. Stairs ascend to an upper room, the site of the Passover Seder led by Jesus on the night of the Last Supper. An Israeli flag adds a star of David every year and hangs on a wall. In another corner of the upper room, a Muslim prayer niche discreetly directs Muslims toward Mecca.[9]

Israel was united under King David in the tenth century BC, with seven years in Hebron and forty years in Jerusalem. There he built a palace for his wives and concubines and made plans to build a temple that would house the Ark of the Covenant. Nathan, David's insider prophet, says that the Temple project would be a project for Solomon, David's son by Bathsheba. Nathan is the one who exposes his king as the premeditated murderer of Bathsheba's husband, Uriah the Hittite, whom he ordered his troops to expose in the battle at Ammon's citadel. Nathan relates a parable about the rich owner of flocks of sheep who robs a poor man of his one beloved ewe lamb. When David lashes out at the rich man, the prophet Nathan strikes back:

> ... "You are the man. Thus says the LORD, the God of Israel, 'I anointed you king over Israel, and I delivered you out of the hand of Saul; ... Why have you despised the word of the LORD, to do what is evil in his sight ... For it you did secretly; but I will do this thing before all Israel, and before the sun.'"[10]

Feiler reminds his contemporary readers of the sacred and secular distinctions of David's leadership and the problems when they are fused together:

---

9. Feiler, *Where God was Born*, 84.
10. 2 Sam 12:7, 9, 12 RSV.

[T]he legacy of David's life is as a warning against having again the likes of David, one who attempts to husband profane and sacred power in his own hands. This may be his most startling legacy of all: the first biblical figure that effectively merges church and state becomes the reason that the Bible all but endorses separating church and state. Secular leaders must be strictly curtailed and kept out of spiritual terrain.[11]

Elijah, like Nathan a nonwriting prophet, casts an overwhelming presence beyond his seventh-century-BC lifetime when he defies King Ahab and Queen Jezebel and their lackey prophets at an altar on Mt. Carmel dedicated to pagan gods:

> Elijah took twelve stones, according to the number of the tribes of the sons of Jacob, to whom the word of the LORD came, saying "Israel shall be your name," and with the stones he built an altar in the name of the LORD.[12]
>
> He said, "I have been very jealous for the LORD, the God of hosts; for the people of Israel have forsaken thy covenant, thrown down thy altars and slain thy prophets with the sword; and I, even I only am left."[13]

Seven-thousand like-minded Yahwehists join Elijah's rank-and-file and the house of Ahab and Jezebel will come to an inglorious end (1 Kgs 21:29). An incident during the reign of King Jehoash (835–796 BC) linked a monotheistic revival of the people of Judah with the discovery of the book of the law buried in a wooden chest full of the Tyrian silver coins that the priests collected to pay workmen for Temple repairs (2 Kgs 12:10).

---

11. Feiler, *Where God was Born*, 88.
12. 1 Kgs 18:31–32 RSV.
13. 1 Kgs 19:14 RSV.

Fig. 15—Melqarth Tyrian Shekel

This revival took place after years of apostasy led by former kings and after the division of the single Davidic-Solomonic state into a Northern Kingdom, Israel, and in the south, Judah, including the city of Jerusalem and the Temple. The Temple had fallen into Ba'al worship until the young King Jehoash ordered the chief priest of the Levites to restore the bankrupt sanctuary and to collect funds, now called taxes:

> So the king commanded, and they made a chest, and set it outside the gate of the house of the LORD, And proclamation was made throughout Judah and Jerusalem, to bring in for the LORD the tax that Moses the servant of God laid upon Israel in the wilderness. And all the princes and all the people rejoiced and brought their tax and dropped it in the chest until they had finished.[14]

The book of Daniel is the final text in the canon of the Hebrew Bible. Chapters 1 and 8 to 12 are in Hebrew and chapters 2–7 are in Aramaic. This adds to the mysticism that the prophet experiences while living as an eminent Jewish captive in the palaces of the Babylonian King Nebuchadnezzar and later Persian kings. Daniel undoubtedly understands the Babylonian streetside moneychangers' cry, *"Mene, Mene, Tekel, Parsin."*

---

14. 2 Chr 24:8–10 RSV.

HEBREW DIVINE NAMES

Fig. 16—Mene, Mene, Tekel, Peres

Daniel serves as Nebuchadnezzar's son, Belshazzar's, "chief of the magicians, enchanters and astrologers" (Dan 5:11), and therefore is expected to literally divine the cries of the moneychangers whose barking words are written on the wall at Belshazzar's feast. "Numbered" (*mene*) and "Weighed" (*tekel*, or shekel) and "Divided" (*peres*) is the Babylonian kingdom. His closeness to these potentates leads him to some tough decisions affirming the God of his forefathers. Next he survives the pit for lions, the Zoroastrian ritual of disposing of a body without polluting the air, water, earth, and fire, that extends Daniel's life into the reign of Cyrus the Great (Dan 6:28). Throughout the Aramaic sections, Daniel is the outsider Jew who makes it on the inside with the help of his Most High God. This divine name is recorded half a dozen times along with the ethereal name, Ancient of Days, in the book's seventh chapter. Daniel assumes the role of apocalyptic herald who envisions events beyond his present situation reported in chapters 7–12. These chapters could have been written in the same years as the Aramaic sections (chapters 2–6) or, as some scholars concede, the entire book may describe events during the last three centuries BC, moving surreptitiously from palace to international intrigues. Alexander the Great (356–323 BC) is introduced to Daniel in a deep sleep vision of the Greek warrior's image that appears on coins as a two-horned ram.

Fig. 17—Alexander's Horns Image Coin

The ram batters the Media-Persian Empire into collapsing and four powers appear on the scene when the ram meets his appointed end. King Antiochus IV (175–163 BC), the scion of the Seleucid successors to Alexander's empire, is the object of Daniel's secretive visions. Antiochus's name neither appears in Daniel's texts nor in Matthew's Gospel, where Jesus repeats the phrase "abomination of desolation" (Matt 24:15). Jesus' apocalyptic warnings to his disciples take place below the Temple wall hours before his crucifixion. The final book in the New Testament canon is appropriately called *Apocalypse*, and like Daniel, Revelation is a prophetic book full of obscure symbols pointing to traumatic events.

Antiochus IV, a devotee of Hellenic cultural and religious symbols, has his image minted on coins adding *Epiphanes* ("god manifest"), a self-deification statement imitating the incarnation of the god Zeus.

Fig. 18—Antiochus Epiphanes Coin

His enemies in Judah are incensed even further by the manipulation of the appointment of the Temple high priests, which leads to revolts that grow into a full-scale war led by the Maccabees following the assault on the Temple in December, 167 BC. Historian John Bright records that fateful day.

> An altar of Zeus (probably an image) was set up, and swine's flesh offered thereon. This is the "abomination of desolation" spoken of by Daniel. Jews were compelled to participate in the feast of Dionysius (Bacchus) and the monthly sacrifice in honor of the king's birthday.[15]

The prophet Daniel sees all of the blasphemies coming to an end when God, the Ancient of Days, returns to his throne and will be manifested as one "like a son of man" (Dan 7:9-14). Jesus identifies himself throughout his three-year ministry as the Son of Man. Daniel the Seer's concluding remarks (chapter 12) are notable for his statements on resurrections leading to either everlasting life or contempt, and mentioning an archangel, Prince Michael, who will be with the people during the coming time of trouble. Previously, Michael was instrumental in interpreting the dream sequences of chapter 8.

The discovery of the Qumran caves above the western shore of the Dead Sea in 1947 becomes the greatest affirmation for the entire Jewish Scriptures. The Hebrew Bible, with the exception of the book of Esther, is represented in these manuscripts known today as the Dead Sea Scrolls (DSS). The scribe-priests fled Jerusalem and the Temple precincts before the time of troubles when Roman legions sacked the capital in AD 70, marking the end of the Qumran caves community which was first established about 100 years earlier. Eleven caves provided a home for the occupants' monastic practices and libraries that contained documents that were eventually lost in the rubble or purposely hidden in sand. A hoard of 561 Tyrian Temple coins dating between 126 and 9 BC suggests this was collected from novices when they enrolled in the community. Clay jars were used to store the scroll of Isaiah and hide coins.[16]

---

15. Bright, *History of Israel*, 406–7.
16. VanderKam, *Dead Sea Scrolls Today*, 22.

RENDERING DIVINE NAMES ON COINS

Fig. 19—Dead Sea Scroll Jar

A DSS researcher and editor, James C. VanderKam, introduces Manual of Discipline, a nonbiblical manuscript, as the priests' guide through the coming apocalyptic events. He quotes from Jewish historian Josephus's description of the Essene sect who set up rigid standards for a novice seeking entry into their congregations:

> If it be [the novice's] destiny, according to the judgement of the Priests and multitude of the men of the Covenant,... to enter the Community, his property and earnings shall be handed over to the Bursar of the Congregation who shall register it to his account ...[17]

Psalms is the Hebrew Bible's most represented book in the DSS. VanderKam links Psalm 37 with a charismatic character known as the Teacher of Righteousness. This psalm's DSS commentary refers to an action of Judean King-High Priest Jannaeus (103–76 BC) who hung 800 Pharisees.[18] This wicked priest is watching over the righteous teacher, and the teacher will finally be vindicated, according to Psalm 37:32–34: "The Lord will not abandon him to his power, or let him be condemned when he is

---

17. VanderKam, *Dead Sea Scrolls Today*, 82.
18. VanderKam, *Dead Sea Scrolls Today*, 106.

brought to trial. Wait for the Lord and keep to his way."[19] The verses of this psalm of David offer counsel to the godly to wait for vindication during a time when evil is rampant. Among the promises for those who do wait and remain faithful are a half-dozen references to the land, beginning with verse 3: "Trust in the Lord, and do good; so you will dwell in the land, and enjoy security."[20] Other promises of land for those who wait are found in verses 9, 24, and 34. Jesus might have had this chapter in mind when he offered his Sermon on the Mount about the blessed ones, the meek, inheriting the earth (Matt 5:5). Psalm 37:11 and 22 not only convey patience in time, but also patience in accumulating land, the essence of wealth.

When Psalm 37 was originally composed, the two most common names for God—Elohim and YHWH—Lord, were virtually interchangeable, and tied to the people of Israel, who expected their leaders, kings, and priests, to do justice in the land. When the new voices from the prophets cried out, the Lord God moved beyond the original concept of a tribal god to become a universal divinity. King David's status guided the idea of a single human ruler, but the prophets, priests, and preachers remained divided on what would be the way to the Almighty. A native son of Israel would appear unannounced and not remembered by the Jerusalem kings and her Temple priests, but for the prophets, Jesus was worthy of the wait.

---

19. Ps 37:33–4 RSV.
20. Ps 37:3 RSV.

3

Gospels of Jesus Christ

*Kerygma of the Incarnation
and Kingdom of God*

PROCLAMATION. HERALD. HORN. FROM the days of Homer, all three words originate from *karuz,* or sea shell, which served as a trumpet for the watchman on the wall signaling the approach of friendly troops with the good news of victory. Any bad news would result in a devastating proclamation by the *herald* blowing a horn. The *shofar,* ram's horn, is blown by seven priests on the seventh and last march around Jericho. Joshua ordered his Israelite forces to shout the good news that the Lord delivered Jericho into their hands (Josh 6:16). The horn takes on a different meaning when the horn is *qarn,* an animal horn. The vision described by the prophet Daniel in Susa (Dan 8:1–6) is of a two-horned ram. The Hebrew word, *qarn,* morphed into Aramaic and then into Arabic when Alexander the Great (see Fig. 17) was identified as the possessor of doubled horns, *Dhul-Qarnain in Qur'an* (Surah 18:86).

The birth of Jesus Christ is implied in Hebrew texts and is explicit in two announcements in two gospels of the Greek Bible. The Prophet Isaiah (Isa 7:14) is the source for the Gospel of Matthew's proclamation: "Behold a virgin shall conceive and bear a son, and his name shall be called Emmanuel (which means, God with us)."[1] The Gospel of Luke's opening chapter features Mary, the mother of Jesus, hearing the angel proclaim that she, Mary, "will conceive in your womb and bear a son, and you shall call his name Jesus. He will be great, and will be called the Son of the Most High."[2] The Qur'an devotes much of Surah 19, titled *Maryam,* to the births of John the Baptist

1. Matt 1:23 RSV.
2. Luke 1:31–32 RSV.

and Jesus, the Son of Mary, but never as the Son of God. The Gospels of Mark and John have no birth narratives, but John testifies that the Word, Jesus, came into the world as an incarnational event: "And the Word became flesh and dwelt [tabernacled] among us, full of grace and truth; we have beheld his glory, glory as the only Son from the Father."[3] How this God-in-the-flesh breaks into human history was recently explored by an astrophysicist who examines a first-century coin and its connection with the birth of Jesus.

A bronze coin features a leaping ram that turns his head to look back at a star. The coin was minted in Antioch, Syria, from AD 5–11, and is the subject of a recent book by Michael Molnar, astrophysics professor and numismatist.[4]

Fig. 20—Antioch Ram, Star Coin

Molnar unravels some of the mysteries of the magi who appear at the birth of Jesus, according to Matthew. The magi, *magoi*, inquire about the birth of a king:

> "Where is he who has been born king of the Jews? For we have seen his star in the East, and have come to worship him". . . Then Herod summoned the wise men secretly and ascertained from them what time the star appeared; and he sent them to Bethlehem, saying, "Go and search diligently for the child, and when you have found him bring me word, that I too may come and worship him." When they had heard the king they went on their way; and lo, the star which they had seen in the East went before them, till it came to rest over the place where the child was. When they saw the star, they rejoiced exceedingly with great joy; and going into

---

3. John 1:14 RSV.
4. Molnar, *Star of Bethlehem*, 14.

the house they saw the child with Mary his mother, and they fell down and worshiped him. Then, opening their treasures, they offered him gifts, gold, frankincense, and myrrh. And being warned in a dream not to return to Herod, they departed to their own country by another way.[5]

The search for the king-star directing the magi to Bethlehem leads Molnar to explore the eclipse of the planet Jupiter at dawn on April 17, 6 BC, in the constellation Aries. Aries, another name for the Ram, was the Judean sign in the Zodiac system (*zodiakos kuklos*, or "circle of animals").[6] As counselors to Zoroastrian kings, the magi foretold when a king would be born and this was relevant for Judea during any eclipse. Matthew reassured his Jewish-Christian readers living in Antioch after AD 55 that Jesus was the Messiah while they physically held coins with the Ram and star images. The Gospel of Matthew account is of the royal birth, heralded by the magi kingmakers bearing gifts from kings to a newborn king. In the Gospel of Luke, Jesus' birth is announced by angels to humble shepherds in fields with their flocks. Matthew follows the magi's visit to the child and the issues arising from the king-star's appearance. Molnar remarks:

> Biblical scholars have noted the mysteriousness of the star described in Matthew. The star ostensibly appears in the east and moves before the magi as they travel from the east, a seeming physical contradiction. Then, the star amazingly stands above the child, an apparently unusual celestial event. There is no reason to doubt that the magi came from the east of Judea, where astrology was practiced. But the puzzle is about a star "in the east," a phrase that in a literal translation means to some people that the star was behind the magi as they traveled west to Judea. Other people believe that the magi followed the star that "went before" them. All of this confusion is the result of thinking like a modern person and not like an astrologer of antiquity.[7]

The magi astrologers/astronomers were able to see the Star of Bethlehem on their charts in the Parthian capital, Ctesiphon, a city noted for studies of the heavens, and for the births and deaths of rulers. From a German church we have a stone sculpture of three sleeping magi under the star

---

5. Matt 2:2, 7–12 RSV.
6. Molnar, *Star of Bethlehem*, 47–48.
7. Molnar, *Star of Bethlehem*, 87.

which humorously illuminates the Molnar thesis. The magi only saw the star on their charts but after they woke up they went to Bethlehem.

Fig. 21—Three Sleeping Magi

The Parthian and Roman Empires also slept comfortably during a truce allowing the magi safe passage across disputed desert borderlands. The Parthian kingdom was ruled by Phraataces at the time of Jesus' birth. This small nation was noted for prolonged resistance to Roman expansion into the Mesopotamia region after which Palmyra became a model Roman city in the eastern Syrian desert. Augustus Caesar maintained the Mediterranean as a Roman sea and extended a timely peace for the birth of Jesus.

Fig. 22—Parthian King, Goddess Tyche

Fig. 23—Augustus Antioch Mint Coin

Jesus announces good news in the Hebrew Bible when he issues his public proclamation in a Nazareth synagogue by reading from the prophet Isaiah.

> "The Spirit of the Lord is upon me, because he has anointed me to preach good news to the poor. He has sent me to proclaim release to the captives and recovering of sight to the blind, to set at liberty those who are oppressed, to proclaim the acceptable year of the Lord."[8]

The Hebrew word *qara* (proclaim) is translated *karuz* in the Greek New Testament and then problematically *karuz* is translated into the English verb "preach." Another term that is closer to the original herald-with-horn of classical Greek k-e-r happens to be *kerygma* with *yg* replacing the z sound with *ma* ending. *Kerygma* and *karusso* are interchangeable for "public proclamation," not only in the gospels, but also in a letter of Paul. The apostle appeals to his readers with a self-reference as a *karuz* in his letter to his disciple Timothy: "For this gospel [good news] I was appointed a herald [karuz preacher], apostle and teacher."[9] The Gospels of Matthew and Luke cite Jesus' comment on the prophet Jonah when he mentions the sign of Jonah as a sign of repentance by the men of Nineveh who repented at the preaching (*kerygma*) of Jonah (Matt 12:41). Both Matthew and Luke recall how the Queen of Sheba's visit to King Solomon's court relates to the subject of repentance. Matthew ends the narrative by stating, "Something greater than Jonah is here." Luke repeats the Matthew rendering, then adds, "Something greater than Solomon is here" (Luke 11:31). Typically

8. Luke 4:18 RSV.
9. 2 Tim 1:11 RSV.

greater-than statements infer preeminence, which means that Jesus' glory overwhelms both Solomon's and Jonah's glorious and miraculous stories of redemption. The subject of repentance, however, is an intentional word of hope for all humankind and comprises the global evangelistic component to Jesus' kerygmatic teaching summarized in Matthew. Jesus declares that God authorized his Son's power when Jesus delivers what is known as the Great Commission. He addresses his eleven disciples in Galilee thusly:

> "Go therefore and make disciples of all nations, baptizing them in the name of the Father and the Son and of the Holy Spirit, teaching them to observe all that I have commanded you; and lo, I am with you always, to the close of the age."[10]

Jesus' heavenly Father is affectionately addressed in what will be known as the Lord's Prayer that opens with *Abba*, "Father," "Papa," a child's cry to an all-embracing parent.

> "Pray then like this: Our Father who art in heaven,/Hallowed be thy name. Thy kingdom come,/Thy will be done,/On earth as it is in heaven./Give us this day our daily bread;/And forgive us our debts,/As we also have forgiven our debtors;/And lead us not into temptation,/But deliver us from evil."[11]

Hallowing or making the name sacred comes by recognizing the holiness, the unfathomable differences, separating the Creator from his creation. Moses faced the Holy God in Sinai, where even the ground was sacred, when he heard the voice at the burning of the bush (Exod 3:3–5). During the Exodus, Moses prays for his people who have been bitten by fiery serpents and are dying in the region of Edom east of the Dead Sea. Near the end of his earthly days, Moses is told by the Lord to create a bronze serpent, placing it on a pole, on which the reptile seemingly coils upward, offering redemption to the people. John, the author of the fourth gospel, writes about the bronze serpent: "And as Moses lifted up the serpent in the wilderness, so must the Son of Man be lifted up, that whoever believes in him may have eternal life."[12]

---

10. Matt 28:19–20 RSV.

11. Matt 6:9–13 RSV. Ancient authorities add this, "For thine is the kingdom and the power and the glory, forever. Amen."

12. John 3:14–15; Num 21:4–9 RSV.

Fig. 24—Serpent on Pole, Mt. Nebo, Jordan

The parent-child relationship flips to a debtor-creditor one with the word *debts* (Matt 6:12), a word that better translates the Aramaic word (*hobah*) than "sins" (Luke 11:2). The Jews of first-century, Second-Temple Judah were an indebted people, mostly to the tax collectors representing the Roman-backed Herodians, but also to landlords and Temple tax agents. It is easier to ask forgiveness from tax collectors. Much more grace is needed to forgive one who owes you something. Questions arise in Capernaum in the Galilee area about Jesus and his disciples not paying taxes (Matt 17:24–27). The collectors for the half-shekel Temple tax ask Peter about his Master's duties as a Jew to pay this annual tax. Jesus and Peter have a private conversation regarding this census tax that originated in the wilderness days. The priests were authorized by Moses to assess adult males for repairs on the Temple (Exod 30:11–16). The Tyrian silver shekel (see Fig 15) would pay the assessment for two adults. This was the catch when Peter, directed by Jesus, glanced inside a fish that he hooked in the Sea of Galilee. There he would discover the Temple tax coin—The Melqarth Tyrian silver!

Days later, Jesus is with his disciples in the Jerusalem Temple where he is approached by representatives of the Pharisees and Herodians. Another silver coin suddenly appears. The tax investigators begin:

> "Teacher, we know that you are true, and teach the way of God truthfully, and care for no man; . . . Tell us, then, what you think. Is it lawful to pay taxes to Caesar, or not?" But Jesus, aware of their malice, said, "Why put me to the test, you hypocrites? Show me the money for the tax." And they brought him a coin. And Jesus said to them, "Whose likeness and inscription is this?" They said, "Caesar's." Then he said to them, "Render therefore to Caesar the things that are Caesar's and to God the things that are God's."[13]

Stardom as a divine Augustus Caesar was relatively new for Tiberius following the death of his stepfather, the Great Augustus Caesar in 14 AD. Historian Bruce Winter mentions that the newly installed Tiberius apparently was wavering about his divine qualifications. However, Tiberius was urged to identify himself with the fame of his stepfather, Augustus, and grandfather, Julius Caesar, which would designate Tiberius as *Divus Augustus*.[14] The new Caesar's wife, Livia, who also has divine status, appears on the reverse side of a denarius coin that was picked from one of the questioner's pockets. This Temple coin, or "penny," pictured with the two Roman gods, met the qualifications to pay the Temple tax, just as the god Melqarth shekel was trusted to have the correct weight of silver coin that met the Temple standard (see Fig. 15). Jesus' answer amazed the religious, legalistic Pharisees and the politically savvy Herodians that Caesar and God both need to be rendered to and honored throughout the Roman world. This answer has continued to bewilder sacred and secular legalists throughout human history.

---

13. Matt 22:16–21 RSV.

14. Winter, *Divine Honours for the Caesars*, 62, 79–81.

Fig. 25—Caesar Tiberius Denarius Coin

Tiberius's cheek bears a crescent-shaped test mark applied by some government official or merchant, testing that the coin was not debased (i.e., was of solid silver and not just a silver veneer with a valueless copper core). Roman economic issues caused by inflation, wars, and silver availability affected the coins' susceptibility to these punched marks (see Fig. 09).

Money and debts are familiar subjects in the parables that Jesus adopts as a teaching style, beginning with the Parable of the Sower in Matthew 13. The sower and cognate parables in other gospels talk about the seed on the barren ground choked by *riches* (v. 22) and the good seed producing a harvest of thirty, sixty, and 100 times the single seed planted in the good ground (v. 23). The parable of the loss of one sheep out of a flock of 100 (Matt 18:12) with a parallel parable in Luke 15 about a lost and found coin and a lost son, reveal more than monetary values for their owners. In the run-up to his journey to Jerusalem, Jesus tells the parable of the unjust steward whose lord forgives him the debt of 10,000 talents, today's equivalent of 100,000 dollars. The steward showed no pity for minor debts owed to him. Finally, the lord delivers the steward to the jailers until the debt is paid. The morality issue is stated in the final verse: "So also my heavenly Father will do to every one of you, if you do not forgive your brother from your heart (Matt 18:35). Inside the Jerusalem Temple is where Jesus asks his critics why they respect the gold of the Temple more than the Temple itself.[15] Later the disciples comment on the beauty of the Temple, to which Jesus replies with a reference to the prophet Daniel:

> Truly, I say to you, there will not be left one stone upon another that will not be thrown down... So when you see the desolating

---

15. Matt 23:2, 16–17 RSV.

sacrilege spoken of by the prophet Daniel, standing in the holy place (let the reader understand) then let those in Judea flee to the mountains.[16]

A day after this exchange with his disciples, Jesus notices a poor widow who approaches the treasury, (in Greek *gazophulakion*, a cabinet or box at the Temple entrance for offerings, [Luke 21:1–2]).

Fig. 26—Widow's Mite in Temple

She casts two tiny low-mintage coins, *prutot,* in this wooden box (see note at end of chapter—*Prices and Values of New Testament Coins*). When the rich cast their silver coins, the noise alone could have caught Jesus' attention, and he speaks to his disciples of the contrast between the heavy givers and this woman's pittance: "For they all contributed out of their abundance; but she out of her poverty has put in everything she had, her whole living."[17]

Jesus' warnings led his followers prior to AD 70 to flee Jerusalem before Titus' Roman legions literally stripped the Temple of all its gold vessels, as well as the gold-seamed walls. Prior to the final destruction of Jerusalem, the Jews minted their own silver coins proclaiming *shekel of Israel* with a chalice on the coin's obverse, and on the reverse, *Jerusalem [the] holy* with three pomegranates.

16. Matt 24:2, 16–17 RSV.
17. Mark 12:44 RSV.

Fig. 27—Jewish War Silver Half Shekel 66/67 AD

In Rome, Vespasian was robed in Caesarian purples leaving Titus, his son, to successfully put down the Jewish revolt. He was admired as an able caesar dedicated to rebuilding Jerusalem after a series of civil wars. A sketch of a coin issued before Vespasian died in AD 79 shows him standing under a palm tree where a weeping Jewess is kneeling.

Fig. 28—Judaea Capita, Weeping Jewess

A second revolt against the Romans begins in AD 132 when Simon Bar Kochba (Son of the Star) announces his messiahship. The Second Revolt shekel obverse shows four columns of the Temple, and inside, a feature that has been tentatively identified as the ark and the table of showbread. This coin's reverse states: *For the freedom of Jerusalem*. The façade of the Temple is only a wistful memory of the Herodian building destroyed over sixty years earlier in AD 70. Other than the ark's furnishings, an alternative proposal of the Temple's interior actually would be a treasury furnishing, a chest, which was first crafted when the reformer King Jehoash ordered the Temple priests to renew the collection of funds for its repairs (2 Kgs 12:5–16). King Jehoash commissioned the high priest to collect, secure, and deliver the money to the Temple workmen:

> Then Jehoiada the priest took a chest, and bored a hole in the lid of it, and set it beside the altar on the right side as one entered the house of the LORD; and the priests who guarded the threshold put in all the money that was brought into the house of the LORD. . .Then they would give the money that was weighed out into the hands of the workmen. . .and they paid it out to the carpenters and the builders who worked upon the house of the LORD.[18]

The Bar Kochba combatants' overwhelming concern would be collecting funds for their guerrilla wars against Rome, and the chest for the coins would graphically remind them of the cost for the liberation of their city and nation. The chest's bored holes, purposes, and location deserves a second biblical archaeological search.[19]

Fig. 29—Bar Kochba Revolt Coin 135 AD

The Roman Emperor Hadrian rebuilt the city, renaming it Aelia Capitolina, where he dedicated a temple to Jupiter. Gentiles and Christians, but not Jews, were allowed to return to Jerusalem, adding to hostilities between the two faiths at an early stage of Christian history.

John's Gospel reduces Jesus' three-year public ministry to twenty days of miraculous signs heralding the message of salvation and, on several occasions, introducing specific names to disclose his personal ministry: "I am the bread of life" (6:35), "the light of the world" (8:1), "door to the sheep"

---

18. 2 Kigs 12:9, 11 RSV.
19. Hendin, *Cultural Change*, 52.

(10:7), "good shepherd" (10:11), "resurrection and the life" (11:25), "the way, the truth, and the life" (14:6), and "the true vine" (15:1). These seven "I am" statements differ from the Caesarian coins that simply added a one word attribute expressing some pious ideal, such as "concord," "equity," or "justice." Resurrection is on the mind of Lazarus' sister Martha when Jesus proclaims, "I am the resurrection and the life." Jesus, the true vine, desires his disciples to know that he is dynamically attached to each of them, even in the face of his impending, crushing death. John's Gospel also reports an intimate meeting with his twelve disciples, including his betrayer, Judas Iscariot. On this night of his arrest, John, the beloved disciple and gospel writer, has Jesus calmly speaking in what later mystics will call the language of the heart when dealing with his separation and coming death (chapters 13–18). Mark's Gospel has several disparate endings that act like counter-marks on coins in that they recertify the original message (Mark 16:9–19) with borrowings from the other gospels. The alternative endings provide hints of what was on the mind of Mark's early Christian readers. The shortest of these alternative endings is added to verse 8 of chapter 16.

> But they reported briefly to Peter and those with him all that they had been told. And after this, Jesus himself sent out by means of them, from east to west, the sacred and imperishable proclamation of eternal salvation.[20]

The proclamation, defined here by Jesus' *kerygma*, pays homage to Peter, which hints of some tensions within the church regarding apostolic leadership. Also, the reference "from east to west" aligns with another addition to Mark 14 and with the Gospel of Matthew, which is Jesus' final proclamation at his ascension. Mark's Gospel adds these words later to validate Matthew's Great Commission text.

> And he said to them, "Go into all the world and preach the gospel to the whole creation. He who believes and is baptized will be saved; but he who does not believe will be condemned."[21]

These recorded words of Jesus, including the command to be baptized, were once thought to be fully vetted by the first-century church. However, the opposite is more accurate when it came to the spirited creedal discussions about the theology of the Father, Son, and Holy Spirit during the next five centuries. The birth of Jesus sets the calendar demarcations of BC and

---

20. Mark 16:8 RSV.
21. Mark 16:15 RSV.

AD that come close to the eclipse noted by the magi in 6 BC. The incarnation date (BC/AD) will not be stamped on coins until the year 1251, when Arabic-speaking Christians in Acre surreptitiously minted a coin mentioning that their ruling king's authority was Jesus. This undated gold bezant, a dinar coin, has a crudely stamped cross in the center. It is an imitation of an Egyptian Fatimid coin, but minted in Acre by the Crusader Kingdom of Jerusalem (see Appendix A).

Fig. 30—Kingdom of Jerusalem Coin

Prices and Values of New Testament Era
(courtesy of David Hendin[22])

The shekel denomination is equivalent to the *tetradrachm*. It is made up of four quarters, called *drachm* or *denarius* (plural, *denarii*). Each shekel contained around 456 bronze prutah coins (plural *prutot*), a number that varied during different periods.

We can better understand the value of these coins by exploring the New Testament, Josephus, and rabbinical sources such as the Talmud. For example:

- Wages: In the early first century, Rabbi Hillel's daily wage was one-half *denarius*. A good scribe earned twelve *denarii* per week. Scribes were paid a few *prutot* to write each normal document.
- Bread: In the first and second centuries CE, a loaf of bread cost around sixteen *prutot*, while a small loaf cost only eight *prutot*.
- Olive oil: Josephus reported that one amphora of olive oil from Galilee cost one *drachm* or one *denarius*.
- Fruit: In the first to second centuries CE, the price of one pomegranate was between one and eight *prutot*. A cluster of grapes or figs cost eight *prutot*, and a cucumber, a rare delicacy, cost a *denarius*.
- Livestock: In the first to second centuries CE, an ox cost 100 *denarii*, but a calf cost only twenty *denarii*. A new-born donkey cost two to four *denarii*, as did a lamb. In Jerusalem, two sparrows cost around fourteen *prutot*.
- The cheapest meal for a bridegroom, who would surely dine lavishly, cost one *denarius*, but a modest meal of a small roll, a plate of lentils, two pieces of meat, and two glasses of wine cost around twenty *prutot*.
- Several oil lamps and wicks cost only one *prutah*.

In ancient times, as today, inflation and the laws of supply and demand moved prices to comparable commodities at different times.

---

22. Hendin, *Cultural Change*, 113.

4

Greet the New Smiths

*Paul, Priscilla, and Aquila: Tabernaclemakers,
Not Tentmakers*

ARCHAEOLOGISTS UNCOVERED A SILVER object in a cave on the slope of Jerusalem's Hinnom Valley during the 1979–80 digging season. This artifact, an amulet, was identified as a charm worn to wear on one's body to ward off evil. The less-than-four-inch-long silver object, once unrolled, revealed the earliest recorded Hebrew Bible inscriptions. Gabriel Barkay reviews this momentous find in a 2009 edition of *Biblical Archaeology Review*.[1]

---

1. Barkay, "Riches of Ketef Hinnom," 22–35.

Fig. 31—Silver Amulet Biblical Blessings

The amulet relates the passage in Numbers 6:24 where the Lord speaks directly to Moses, asking Aaron and his sons, the priests, as well as the people Israel to plead for the Lord's blessing on them.[2]

The delicate engraving skill of these ancient Hebrew words and the challenging task of unfolding the thin silvery sheets are worthy of an extended study. However, this chapter's more limited objective is to introduce Paul and his Jewish colleagues, Priscilla and Aquila, as the creators of mini-tabernacles, similar to this sixth-century-BC amulet and to designate this missionary team as silversmiths rather than tentmakers, the universally accepted interpretation of the Greek, *skanopoios*. The word is only found once in the Bible, in Acts 18:3, when Paul arrives in Corinth and meets this Judeo-Christian husband-and-wife team who had been recently expelled from Rome by Emperor Claudius in AD 50 because of their Jewish background. When Paul sends greetings, he refers to Priscilla as Prisca in Ephesus (1 Cor 16:19). In another epistle, Paul greets Prisca first and Aquila secondly (2 Tim 4:19). The reason why Paul shortened Priscilla's name and

2. Num 6:24 RSV.

elevated her above Aquila are only hinted at, but her adeptness at designing coins and jewelry must be considered.

The Greek word, *skanopoios*, consists of a first syllable of three consonants, *skn*, and a two-syllable ending, *po-ois*, preceded by the connector *o* in the middle. *Poios* is a common Greek word for "worker" or "maker." The Hebrew letters for this term are close to the Greek consonants, *skn*. Biblical languages agree on the basic definition of the words formed by *skn* that translates as "dwelling" or "home." Impressively, the *shkn* consonants which appear several times in Exodus 40:34–36 specifically relate to the wilderness wanderings for the Tabernacle and the smaller tentlike dwellings of the people. When the Greek word *skanopoios* becomes "tabernaclemakers," the religious history of Israel becomes apparent. Conversely, what possible service could Paul and his coevangelists perform that allowed them entry into synagogues and provide a marketable skill during Paul's multiple itinerations throughout the northeastern Mediterranean basin?

Records from the Babylonian Talmud of the Great Synagogue in Alexandria, Egypt, state that the chief seats in this temple were reserved for these professions: "goldsmiths, silversmiths, blacksmiths, and metal workers."[3] Although this Talmud is a third-century-AD document, it undoubtedly reflects the situation of earlier centuries when Jews in the diaspora comprised a significant population. Unlike their fellow Jews in Judah, who were predominantly peasants, the diaspora Jews were urban dwellers and mostly engaged in professional careers. Early synagogues were often no more than spaces in homes providing a shelf or dedicated wall niches for scrolls containing the words of Moses. This sacred space featured copies of articles that were first introduced to Moses at the beginning of the wilderness journey such as the Table for the Bread of Presence (Levi 24:5–9). The goblet for wine as a symbol of Judaism does not appear until the Jewish war coins in AD 68 (see Fig. 27). For Christians, the cup became a sign of suffering and is established by all four gospels and repeated in Paul's first letter to the Corinthians (1 Cor 11:23–29). The cupboards near the altar space are known as "tabernacles" in the Roman Catholic Church, and as "bread carriers" in the Greek Orthodox churches.

---

3. Feldman, "Palestinian and Diaspora Judaism," 27.

Fig. 32—Tabernacle Shelf in Liturgical Churches

Paul's defense of his ministry regarding his earnings is based on a rabbinic tradition and his claim of freedom to offer the gospel freely (1 Cor 9:18). In this letter (9:1) he answers questions regarding his "workmanship" as those whom he brought to faith in Jesus. Tabernacle-making is a part-time artisan skill that melds into Paul's evangelism goal of "becoming all things to all men in order to win some" (1 Cor 9:22). This passion is implied in references in the Acts of the Apostles and the two Corinthian letters, the same biblical books which introduce Prisca and Aquila, who "worked with their own hands" (1 Cor 4:12) while in Ephesus, a key city where this team settled for about three years during Paul's third missionary journey after AD 55. Paul admonishes his "babes in Christ" to avoid being dependent on any one spiritual leader, including the gifted Apollos and even himself, as the founder of the Corinthian church (1 Cor 3:1). He questions the wayward Corinthians, and then provides his own answer:

> What then is Apollos? And what is Paul? Servants through whom you believed, as the Lord assigned to each. I planted, Apollos watered, but God gave the growth.[4]

Paul's use of agricultural metaphors turns to something less natural, from God's field to God's building (v. 9). He then inserts himself into the building trade where the workers are his wages and he becomes the architect (v. 10). "According to the commission of God given to me, like

---

4. 1 Cor 3:5–6 RSV.

a skilled master builder I laid a foundation."[5] The skilled master builder (Greek *architekton*), high tech(nician), takes his payment as investment in souls and likely his real wages in building foundations. "For no other foundation can anyone lay than. . . Jesus Christ. Now if anyone builds on the foundation with gold, silver, precious stones, wood, hay or stubble. . ."[6] Descriptions of the foundation here have led to expositions on the Temple of Solomon which is a negative image of precious ores and gems being buried in a foundation. These metals were visible inside the wilderness tabernacle, as well as in the Jerusalem Temples. While the beauty of the metals and stones was a decorative, foundational component, how did the wood, hay, and stubble contribute to the basic product? That may be extracted from the next sentence on the heels of verse 12.

> [E]ach man's work will become manifest; for the Day will disclose it, because it will be revealed with fire, and the fire will test what sort of work each one has done.[7]

Fires produced by kindling wood, stubble, and hay are more than just foundational byproducts. The heat can be used to alloy gold and silver, as well as precious stones that are added to the cooled metal in the fashioning of fine jewelry. The subject of the Temple arises when Paul asks another rhetorical question:

> Do you not know that you are God's temple and that God's Spirit dwells in you? If any one destroys God's temple, God will destroy him. For God's temple is holy, and that temple you are.[8]

Paul consoles his faltering Corinthian converts with overwhelming praises when he writes, "You embody a holy temple" (1 Cor 3:17). In a conciliatory second letter to the Corinthians less than a year later, Paul emphasizes the indwelling Spirit, but this time he uses the metaphor of a tabernacle, which is interchangeable with "temple":

> For we know that if the earthly tent [*skanous*] we live in is destroyed, we have a building from God, a house not made with hands, eternal in the heavens. Here indeed we groan and long to

---

5. 1 Cor 3:10 RSV.
6. 1 Cor 3:11–12 RSV.
7. 1 Cor 3:13 RSV.
8. 1 Cor 3:16–17 RSV.

RENDERING DIVINE NAMES ON COINS

put on our heavenly dwelling... He who has prepared us for this very thing is God, who has given us the Spirit as a guarantee.[9]

Paul uses a commercial word to describe the Holy Spirit, the deposit, the first installment on a purchase. The word, *arrabona,* is only found here and in Ephesians 1:14, identifying Jesus Christ as the pledge for full ownership later. There is a cluster of financial words that appear in his Philippians letter (4:15–18) where Paul is attempting to balance the books into debt and credit columns. His business Greek vocabulary demonstrates that he remained in contact with members of a commercial group during the missionary journeys and later while he was in prison.

The book of Acts tells how Paul links up with Prisca and Aquila in Corinth, where the recently exiled couple had secured a house. Paul resides in this house where the trio worked their trade in making tabernacles, and Paul spent his Sabbaths convincing both Jews and gentile-Greeks to follow the way of Jesus (Acts 18:1–4). The physician and part-time fellow traveler, Luke, records this final word from Acts about Paul's open-house policy in Rome prior to his death in AD 62:

> And [Paul] lived [in Rome] two whole years at his own expense and welcomed all who came to him, preaching the kingdom of God and teaching about the Lord Jesus Christ quite openly and unhindered.[10]

Based upon their specific skill-set, working with precious metals, it is more than plausible that the three would be qualified silversmiths attached to a local mint for minting silver coins under Roman authorities, who firmly regulated the mining of silver and the minting of coins. Further, it will be assumed that these Jewish smiths are Roman citizens which Paul claims on several occasions (Acts 23:27). The heavy lifting is done by slaves who mine the veins of silver while other skilled slaves labor in house-shop quarters, pounding the metal, billowing the kilns, extracting the billon, and weighing the coins.

---

9. 2 Cor 5:1, 2, 5 RSV.
10. Acts 28:30–31 RSV.

Fig. 33—Cupid's Mint on Pompeii Wall

The high-tech skills are in the designing of the coins' faces and preparing the dies to strike the ruling Caesars' and goddesses' bust profiles on the heated metals. There were hundreds of these household mints throughout the Roman Empire during the first century when Rome gave independent statuses to Greek city-states like Philippi, Antioch, Corinth, and Ephesus. Tarsus was central to the making of the Roman coin dies and where Paul undoubtedly learned his high-tech crafts and his citizenship from his own forebears.

Paul's trip to Jerusalem and back to Ephesus is tracked by Luke in Acts 18:24—19:10. Priscilla and her husband meet in Ephesus with Apollos as part of Paul's mission to the Jews, starting in the synagogues. Luke doubles down with the remarkable claim that the gospel was dispersed throughout the entire province of Asia (Acts 19:10, 26). The first half of this Acts chapter ends with a conflict between Paul and some Jewish exorcists who try to imitate some of the miracles that Paul performed. The struggle concludes when several of these exorcists confessed Jesus as Lord and surrendered their books on magic arts to public burning: "[T]hey counted the value of the books and found it came to fifty thousand pieces of silver. So the word of the Lord grew and prevailed mightily."[11] There is a major reaction from the local Ephesian silversmiths who have a lucrative business associated with the temple of Artemis. The remaining half of chapter 19 conveys the intrigue and violence instigated by the silversmiths against the Jews and Paul's disciples. Paul departs the city safely, helped by the local Roman officials who Luke identifies as Asiarchs and "friends" of Paul (v. 31). These friends and the town clerk who speaks out as a mayor not only control the mob, but interpret this uprising as a mercantile problem unrelated to religion or idolatry. The crowd rioting in the Ephesian amphitheater has no clue what the issues are. Would some cry out with the words that Pontius

---

11. Acts 19:19 RSV.

Pilate heard from the mob at the trial of Jesus? "You are not Caesar's friend!" (John 19:12) The two government officials shout back that there is no blasphemous denunciation of Artemis coming from Paul. The disputations and confusion are likely tied to the huge amount of money (v. 19), the 50,000 silver *drachmas,* which is equivalent today to millions of dollars. There is no money exchanged, but the threat is real for the silversmiths who fear that Paul and his partners will corner the silver market if that amount of money falls into the hands of artisans designing, minting, and selling shrine-like pieces like the mini tabernacles. Luke finds the proverbial silver lining in this disturbance, during which Paul is charged by the silver tradesmen for propagating his anti-Artemis message. That disruptive commercial message and Paul's gospel message are both amplified throughout the province of Asia and throughout the world (Acts 19:20, 27).

Paul, Prisca, and Aquila, as makers of silver tabernacles, continue their greater objective of presenting the kingdom of God message to Jews and gentiles. Their mint-houses serve as jewelry stores as well as worship centers. The ruins of Pompeii, following the eruption of Mount Vesuvius in AD 79, provide a glimpse of the production amulets. Archaeologists uncovered a Pompeii shop where gold *bulla* (amulets) were made for Roman citizens who wore them around their necks.

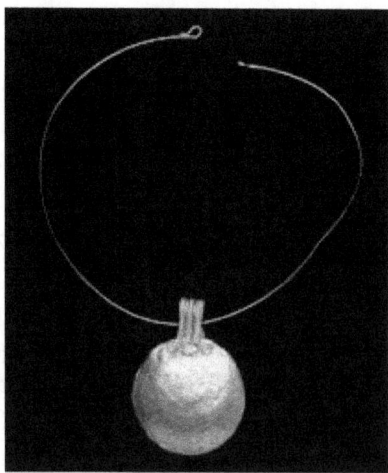

Fig. 34—Gold Bulla Liberty Symbol

Amulets, according to the editors of a Pompeii study, were necklaces that identified the wearers—children, men, and women—as Roman citizens. The gem-cutters who lived in a house on a well-known Pompeii street included a goldsmith metal-engraver (*caelator*) named Priscus, whose tools were recovered along with hundreds of precious gems in the ashes of that Pompeii house. The listed gems were carnelian, sardonyx, amethyst, and agate.[12]

How this multitasking ministry worked is depicted by two widely circulated Greco-Roman coins that Paul routinely handled and possibly was involved in minting. His Galatian letter highlights Christ as the Liberator and the letter to the Romans is a personal appeal for gentiles to honor Paul's Jewish kinfolk. Paul composes Galatians while in Syrian Antioch in the year AD 54/55, and delivers it to the churches of the Asia Minor Galatian region. This was the same year that a newly reissued coin began to circulate among the growing followers who will be called Christians for the first time in Antioch (Acts 11:26). These new disciples looked for bronze coins with Roman dates and the bust of Liberty goddess Tyche on obverse, a leaping ram of the reverse, and on the coin's circular edge in Greek *Anticlion*, Antiochian. The ram's head turns to observe a star in a crescent.

Fig. 35—Bronze Goddess Tyche Coin

The later bronze coins with Tyche (Roman *Fortuna*) commemorate the death of Emperor Augustus who died in AD 14. However, the Jewish and gentile followers of Jesus see the leaping ram and Tyche as signifying something far more relevant than the death of Augustus forty years earlier (see Fig. 20). Michael R. Molnar, the American astronomer, dates this coin to an eclipse that took place April 17, 6 BC and which has been documented

---

12. Ward-Perkins and Claridge, *Pompeii 79*, 109.

by modern scholars.[13] Molnar studied this eclipse, more correctly termed an occultation, calculating that a particular alignment of planets occurred on the morning of April 17. However, it was so low on the horizon that it would not have been visible to observers at the time. Molnar cites a fourth-century scholar looking back at the records of the eclipse:

> [F]or an astrologer to observe this event, the moon and Jupiter must be above the horizon at the moment of closest passage, prerequisites making any visual verification difficult.[14]

The Antioch Christians recognized the planet Jupiter (the ram) as the zodiac sign for Judea, and the crescent moon as the sign of a regal power arising at the death of a ruler. Another numismatic study reveals that the Tyche ram coin in AD 54/55 commemorated the twenty-fifth anniversary of Jesus' death and sixty-year anniversary of his birth.[15] Both Molnar's book and Cartwright's blog based their conclusions on the Gospel of Matthew account of the Zoroastrian magi who arrived in Bethlehem with three gifts for a new ruler. Theologians Martin Hengel and Maria Schwemer have linked coins showing the goddess Tyche with the city of Antioch. In this context, the goddess assumes the role of a liberator:

> "Tell me, you who desire to be under law, do you not hear the law? For it is written that Abraham had two sons, one by a slave and one by a free woman. But the son of the slave was born according to the flesh, the son of the free woman through promise. [Greek *allagoroumena*]. Now this is an allegory: These women are two covenants. One is from Mount Sinai, bearing children for slavery; she is Hagar. Now Hagar is Mount Sinai in Arabia; she corresponds to the present Jerusalem, for she is in slavery with her children. But the Jerusalem above is free, and she is our mother."[16]

The contacts Paul made with synagogues in Syria and Arabia (Damascus southward to Petra) are presented by Hengel and Schwemer, who relate how the city goddess Tyche represents the liberated woman, the unnamed Sarah, in Galatians. Paul's train of thought in this allegory connects Jerusalem above to freedom, which is symbolized by an earthly mother, Sarah, and Hagar is identified with Mount Sinai and slavery under the law. The

---

13. Molnar, *Star of Bethlehem*, 86.
14. Molnar, *Star of Bethlehem*, 107.
15. Cartwright, "Star of Bethlehem Coins," 12.
16. Gal 4:21–26 RSV.

Galatians letter emphasizes Christ as Liberator (5:1), with Paul urging his readers not to submit to slavery. Freedom (*eleutheria* in Greek) from slavery in this Galatian letter means freedom from religious laws, specifically circumcision for the non-Jewish males. This message of freedom will be a topic of sermons he'll preach in synagogues filled with gentiles and Jews. He will also go on record for his right to earn wages apart from donations (1 Cor 9:1, 18). An alternate job opening is reviewed in Ronald F. Hock's 1980 book with the subtitle of *Tentmaking and Apostleship*. The treatise defines Paul as the missionary-tentmaker who is motivated to labor in a sweatshop to fulfill some sacred outreach among the lower classes:

> [Paul] refused to be a financial burden and so found work making tents and other leather products in order to be self-sufficient. Making tents meant rising before dawn, toiling until sunset with leather, knives, and awls, and accepting various social stigmas and humiliations that were part of the artisans' lot, not to mention the poverty...[17]

Hock's main title, *The Social Context of Paul's Ministry*, is supported by a four-page bibliography listing ancient sacred and secular Hebrew and Greek texts in contrast to the slightly-over-one-page list of New Testament texts. In overlooking the basic etymological origins of the word *skanopois* as "tabernacle maker" rather than "tentmaker," Hock's thesis shuts down most of the other qualifications of Paul's unique ministries as an evangelist-minter that this book proposes. Another more recent book suggests that Paul learned his trade as a tentmaker in Arabia, where Hengel and Schwemer state that the precious materials were woven into linen tents for holy purposes.[18] Any use of tent leather materials raises the problem of unclean hides, such as swine, which were banned according to the dietary law of Deuteronomy 14.

The Roman letter calls for a closer look at the Greek coin with another goddess on its face that will provide more material evidence regarding Paul's high-tech career in the minting of coins, and his being a keen observer of the messages that Greek and Roman coins conveyed to readers and nonreaders within the empire. The second Greek coin under consideration has an image of the goddess Athena, whose face has been seen and imitated from Spain to the Indus Valley for over 1,000 years.

---

17. Hock, *Social Context of Paul's Ministry*, 37.
18. Hengel and Schwemer, *Paul between Damascus and Antioch*, 113, 389n590.

Fig. 36—Athenian Silver Tetradrachm Coin

Athena was the patroness of wisdom, agriculture, and the arts, just to name a few of her attributes. She made sacred the serpent and the rooster, but she mostly appears with the owl and wild olive sprig, the Greek national emblem enshrined by Paul in his Romans letter while in Corinth, from AD 56–57. He reaffirms the divine promises to all the offspring of Abraham and what it means to be in Christ.[19] In the Romans letter, Paul, the self-proclaimed apostle to the gentiles, writes to admonish the gentile believers in the imperial capital to respect the original children of Abraham. Paul moves through some difficult Greek prose, seemingly involving the rejection of Israel while maintaining the defense of his apostleship to the gentiles. He digresses into the metaphorical language of food, both edible and ceremonial: "lump of dough, first fruits, root and then branches" (Rom 11:13–24)! There before him, the coin, the symbol of Greece embodied in its very name, Hellene, *elaia*, is the olive tree and its fruit. Paul, the diaspora Jew, is metaphorically a Hebrew coin stamped (*charaktar*) by the Greek culture and transformed into a new character (*charaktar*) symbolized by the wild olive branch grafted into his Semitic roots. His impressions of the wild olive sprig come from this coin's goddess Athena, whose name is stamped on many coins throughout the Mediterranean world along with the three olive leaves stretched across her head. Paul writes to the gentiles in Rome:

> [I]f the root is holy, so are the branches. But if some of the branches were broken off, and you, a wild olive shoot, were grafted in their place to share the richness of the olive tree, do not boast over the branches. If you do boast, remember it is not you that support the root but the root that supports you. You will

---

19. Gal 3:28–29 RSV.

say, "Branches were broken off so that I might be grafted in." That is true. They were broken off because of their unbelief. . .So do not become proud, but stand in awe. . . Note then the kindness and the severity of God; severity to those who have fallen, but God's kindness to you, provided that you continue in his kindness; otherwise, you too will be cut off.[20]

When the letter asks his non-Jewish readers to note the divine kindness (*chrastotato*) and sternness (*'apotomia*), he uses two rare Greek words which were yet common in the Greek Old Testament (Septuagint), and which Paul frequently quotes rather than the older Hebrew text.

Paul's all-inclusive view of existing in Christ is enhanced by what he observes on the Nabataenan King Aretas coins.

Fig. 37—Coin of King Aretas and Queen

The king is named in 2 Corinthians 11:32 where Paul describes his escape from a Damascus prison by being lowered down a wall in a basket. This is the only case where Paul names a contemporary ruler. The image of King Aretas and his wife appear on the coin's reverse. The goddess, Nike, with the olive wreath crown, is on the coin's obverse. During Paul's three years in Arabia, he saw what it meant to be in Christ. "There is neither Jew nor Greek, there is neither slave nor free, there is neither male nor female; for you are all one in Christ Jesus."[21] Living on the eastern fringes of the biblical Palestinian Holy Land, the Nabataenans claimed descent from Abraham through Hagar, and the name Nabaioth after Ishmael's first-born son (Genesis 25:12–13). The Nabataeans spoke a proto-Arabic language, and, like the

20. Rom 11:16b–20 RSV.
21. Gal 3:28 RSV.

Jews, practiced circumcision. Paul's descriptions as neither Jew nor Greek also suggest a *kerygma* that he proclaims as the liberating gospel of Jesus being all-inclusive, neither Jew nor Greek, male nor female. The Nabataean King Aretas (AD 9–40) and his devoted wives, Hulda and Shaqelah, may have been entombed in this famous monument in Petra.

Fig. 38—Petra Rock, Edifice Misnamed Treasury

After a decade of appeals to Rome for his own freedom, Paul died in Rome where his remains were placed in the catacombs.

Fig. 39—Paul's Image in Catacomb Tomb

Unlike Peter, Paul avoided crucifixion because he was a Roman citizen. Paul's martyrdom by the sword was ordered by Nero Caesar Augustus, the emperor, whose coins outshone all former Roman coins in sheer numbers and beauty.[22] A Nero coin that featured Apollo playing the lyre is associated with the burning of Rome and the accusation that Christians were the arsonists.

Fig. 40—Nero With Apollo and Lyre

22. Alves, in Winter, *Divine Honours for the Caesars*, 219.

Nero breaks a tradition by displaying his deification as a living caesar on this coin, wearing a radiated crown. Other caesars received this honor after their deaths.[23] Whatever friendship Paul had hoped for with Nero definitely had ended by the time of Rome's burning. This led to the persecution of Jesus' followers and Paul's death in AD 63/64. A few years after Paul's demise, Nero took his own life.

Paul's last words to his disciple Timothy reflect the apostle's triumphal, heavenly hopes that are inscribed in the midst of some earthly concerns for Timothy to bring his cloak, some books, and parchments. Prisoner Paul adds, "Alexander the coppersmith did me great harm. . . Beware of him yourself, for he strongly opposed our message."[24] Alexander's career as a worker in copper could be translated as a smith working in iron, brass, bronze, or more generally a blacksmith. The Greek word x*alekos* suggests a professional relationship with Paul and a continuous tabernacle- and coin-making enterprise in Ephesus where his disciple, Timothy, as well as Prisca and Aquila, had a workshop connected with the household of Onesiphorus (2 Tim 4:19).

The First Letter to the Corinthians was written about five years before Paul's execution in Rome. The letter, written in Ephesus, contains several personal appeals to the faltering Corinthians to follow Jesus Christ throughout their daily lives. The thirteenth chapter is Paul's statement of self-immolation when he fails to practice unconditional love. "If I speak in the tongues of men and of angels, but have not love, I am a noisy gong or a clanging symbol."[25] The noisy gong is an attempt by translators to describe the original Greek work, *xalkos*, Alex, the copper/bronze/brass maker's name. Bible lexicologists Arndt and Gingrch add the monetary phrase "small change," to their definitions of *xalkos*.[26] Emptying one's pocket of Lincoln coppers may produce some minor noise, but the lightweight first-century coins such as the widow's mite *prutah* (see Fig. 26) would never be heard as a noisy gong. St. Paul states that without Christ's inspiring love, *agape*, one is an empty, throw-away bottle cap. Noiseless. "If I deliver my body to be burned, but have not love, I gain nothing."[27]

---

23. Winter, *Divine Honours for the Caesars*, 62.
24. 2 Tim 4:13–15 RSV.
25. 1 Cor 13:1 RSV.
26. Arndt and Gingrich, *Greek-English Lexicon*, 883.
27. 1 Cor 13:3 RSV.

5

Gnosticism

Abracadabra in Pre-Nag Hammadi Texts

THE APOSTLE PETER'S DENUNCIATION of Simon Magus set in motion centuries of Christian disputes concerning interpretations of Jewish and Christian Gnosticism:

> Now when Simon saw that the Spirit was given through the laying on of the apostles' hands, he offered them money... But Peter said to him, "Your silver perish with you, because you thought you could obtain the gift of God with money!... Repent therefore of this wickedness of yours, and pray to the Lord, that, if possible, the intent of your heart may be forgiven you.[1]

The magic-performer and all-around charlatan, Great Simon, moved from Samaria to Rome where St. Irenaeus of Lyons (d. AD 200) warned the church about his deceptions as the first-century Heretic-in-Chief.[2] In recent years, skepticism has arisen about Simon's accusers who dismissed other nonconforming, heterodox believers in the final BC and first AD centuries. Egypt emerged as the center of Jewish and later Christian offshoots of Gnosticism.

After the founding of the port city of Alexandria, large numbers of Jews were reading the Greek translation of the Hebrew Scriptures. Seventy (*LXX*) or seventy-two Jews, thus *Septuagint*, made the Bible available not only for their co-believers, but for generations of Greek readers from Paul to twenty-first-century scholars. Displaced by the Persian invasions and

---

1. Acts 8:18, 20, 22 RSV.
2. Irenaeus, quoted in Eusebius, *History of the Church*, 86.

distant from the Jerusalem Temple rituals, Jews in Lower Egypt were exposed to a mystic god called *Abraxas*.

Fig. 41—Gnostic God Abraxas

According to C. W. King, this god passed into gnostic writings from Indian Brahman myths.[3] Several drawings based on woodcuttings and jade ornaments of Abraxas sketched in the King book have common dates and graphics with coins circulating along the Indian frontier. A silver bilingual *drachm*, dated 75–70 BC, has Greek and Indian symbols and Abraxas holding a lotus blossom.

3. King, *Gnostics and Their Remains*, 132.

GNOSTICISM

Fig. 42—Indo-Greek Silver Coin

The Abraxas name, as explained by King, is a corruption of the Hebrew *Ha-Brachah*, "The Blessing," with the Greek pronunciation of the Hebrew *Cha* as "X". The India-Brahman influence grew after Alexander's military ventures in the Indus Valley that opened the door for missionary envoys from India to Egypt. The *Dhamma* posted on the Fourteenth Rock in Kandahar names four Greek kings, including Ptolemy II. Although the Ptolemies and Seleucids were Aśoka's contemporaries, their interactions were limited[4] (see Fig. 08). King suggests that the image of serpent legs was symbolic of Moses lifting up the healing serpent in the Sinai wilderness (Num 21:9; John 3:14; see Fig. 24). Another esoteric code word evolved with the Hebrew to Greek corruption of *Ha-Brachah dabar,* "the Blessing speaks," casting a mighty spell, *abracadabra.*[5] The oldest biblical coin was uncovered in Egypt bearing the name of Hezekiah with a Greek owl on obverse and blank reverse. Hezekiah was a priest who migrated to Egypt during the post-Alexandrian years. The Persians designated this coin and the silver gerah *Yehud,* Judah (see Fig. 10).

---

4. Thapar, *Aśoka and the Decline*, 383.
5. King, 250–1.

RENDERING DIVINE NAMES ON COINS

Fig. 43—Egyptian Coin, Hezekiah Governor

Abraxas's name symbolized a beneficent god in several gnostic scrolls crammed into a clay jar and discovered by a Nile Valley peasant in 1945 at Nag Hammadi, Egypt. Fifty-two separate texts, often in fragments, were eventually mended and edited by scholars after protracted squabbles with antique dealers and government officials. Similar bungled actions were replicated after the Dead Sea Scrolls discovery in 1947 by a Palestinian shepherd who tried to market the priceless DSS (see Fig. 19). Bentley Layton sheds scholarly light on the Nag Hammadi manuscripts, which were originally written in Greek with the majority translated into a Coptic script and other local languages before AD 350.[6]

---

6. Layton, *Gnostic Scriptures*, xxv.

GNOSTICISM

Fig. 44—Nag Hammadi Manuscript

Questions surrounding the hasty burial of the scrolls are answered by Elaine Pagels, who contends that the orthodox Christians were threatened by the mysterious gnostics, who in turn responded by literally going underground.[7] Inside a clay pot, hidden in desert sands, the papyrus texts survived over 1,600 years and now are exposed to attentive readership. Pagels's book, *The Secret Gospel of Thomas*, is based upon translations by the gifted scholar Marvin Meyer, whose death is still felt by his associates. Other manuscripts not discovered in Nag Hammadi, but unearthed further north in the Nile Valley, include *Thomas Gospel*, a small treatise in which *Jesus said* introduces scores of Matthew, Mark, and Luke sayings and nonbiblical phrases. The Sower parable in Matthew 13:24 is presented in Layton's translation of the *Thomas Gospel* text:

> Jesus said, Listen, a sower came forth, took a handful, and cast. Now some fell upon the path, and the birds came and picked them out. Others fell upon rock, and they did not take root in the soil, and did not send up ears. And others fell upon thorns, and they choked the seed; and the grubs devoured them. And others fell

7. Pagels, *Beyond Belief*, 97, 177.

RENDERING DIVINE NAMES ON COINS

upon good soil, and it sent up good crops and yielded sixty per measure and a hundred and twenty per measure.[8]

Another saying has no biblical reference.

Jesus said, "Blessed is the lion that the human being will devour so that the lion becomes human. And cursed is the human being that the lion devours; and the lion will become human."[9]

Jesus' "render unto Caesar" statement modifies three gospels' readings.

They showed Jesus a gold coin and said to him, "Caesar's agents are extorting taxes from us." He said to them, "Give unto Caesar the things that are Caesar's, give unto god the things that are god's, and give unto me that which is mine."[10]

Fig. 45—Tiberius Gold Coin

There is evidence that the original disciple, Thomas, the twin, travelled to South India via Edessa in modern Iraq where the *Thomas Gospel* could have been written. A clue to the spread of gnostic ideas from Syriac and later central Asian centers is offered in this verse from the Jesus sayings:

Jesus said, "Blessed is that which existed before coming into being. If you exist as my disciples and listen to my sayings, these stones will minister unto you. Indeed, you have five trees in paradise,

---

8. Layton, *Gnostic Scriptures*, 381. See also the Parable of the Sower (Matt 13:3–8; Mark 4:3; Luke 8:5).

9. Layton, *Gnostic Scriptures*, 381.

10. Layton, *Gnostic Scriptures*, 397.

which do not move in summer or winter whose leaves do not fall. Whoever is acquainted with them will not taste death."[11]

The five trees are interpreted as five life-or-death stages in gnostic traditions, and are associated with the founder of Manichaeism, begun by the prophet Mani, whose missionaries travelled to far-off Mongolian hinterlands for centuries after his death in AD 250.[12]

Translator Hans-Joachim Klimkeit's extensive rendering of Mani's theology involves five trees of life.[13] Gnosticism along the Silk Road added Zoroastrianism, as well as the Asian Buddhist and Hindu religions, to Christianity and Buddhism. Mani's parents were members of a small Jewish-Christian sect, El Kesaites, who practiced ritual baptisms in the Mesopotamian waterways. Mani left this church as a young man, eventually forming a universal body under his disciples' guidance. Baptismal beliefs and practices uncovered from Nag Hammadi included the journey of a Zoroastrian soul that begins with baptism and continues for at least five more baptisms according to the oracle Zostrianos. Layton excerpted this heavily-worn Coptic manuscript that provides information on the baptismal stages in primeval, pre-Genesis existence.

> . . . angels; demons; intellects, souls, living animals, trees, bodies; and what exists prior to these; (namely), what belong to the simple elements of the simple first principles, which exist (both) confusedly (?). . . and unmixed—air, water, earth, number connection. . .[14]

References to air, water, and earth, along with fire, became sacred elements in Zoroastrianism. This manuscript's Coptic script would have been unreadable for ordinary Egyptians when it was copied around AD 350. Layton states that Zostrianos was not Zoroaster's grandson but an anonymous gnostic author of highly charged metaphoric speculations who wrote in Greek.[15] Counterfeits are cursed in other Nag Hammadi manuscripts. However, the biblical character Seth became a favorite among gnostic writers who sought Bible characters to boost links to the Hebrew Scriptures. As

---

11. Layton, *Gnostic Scriptures*, 383.
12. Layton, *Gnostic Scriptures*, 377.
13. Klimkeit, *Gnosis Silk Road*, 348n7.
14. Layton, *Gnostic Scriptures*, 137. All parentheses are Layton's.
15. Layton, *Gnostic Scriptures*, 121, 125n1.

the grandson of Adam, Seth (Gen 4 and 5) was born after the death of Abel and his exemplary life was perceived as an alter ego in several scrolls.

The Egyptian Gospel belongs to a genre of the Nag Hammadi scrolls referred to as Sethian Literature in the Layton book. An antiphonal chant, led by Jesus at a baptismal service, resounds with the seven Hebrew vowel sounds I-E-E-O-Y-O-A.[16] King records another chant of the ineffable name that he traces to ancient Brahman, Hindu, and Tibetan sources. The first sound of the Buddhist mantra AUM or OM is aided by the chanter's sacred beads.[17] Egyptian links with these Oriental faiths were apparent during the Indian Aśoka reign when this AUM incantation was absorbed by the Hebrew word, amen. Jewish mystics, Kabbalists, following the gnostic penchant for the study of numbers, declared the Hebrew consonants forming 'A-M-Y-N' added up to 99 (1+40+ 8+ 50), a precursor to that sacred number.[18]

The Gnostic Bible co-editors, Barnstone and Meyer, offer several of these Sethian narratives. The gnostic John is ridiculed by St. Irenaeus on his list of heretics in *The Secret Book of John* that provided a list of Bible characters ranging from Adam and Eve to James, son of Zebedee. Seth's children are rarely listed and Abraxas is not named by Meyer.[19] The demiurge god, Ialdabaoth, is the counterforce to Abraxas in gnostic dualism. Ialdabaoth, often written Yaldabaoth, is frequently identified with the Hebrew letter *nun* that twists itself into a serpent.[20]

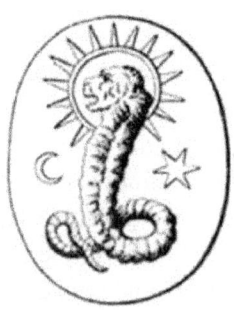

Fig. 46—Ialdabaoth Demiurge God

16. Layton, *Gnostic Scriptures*, 118.
17. King, 266.
18. King, 267.
19. Barnstone and Meyer, *Gnostic Bible*, 135.
20. Layton, *Gnostic Scriptures*, 175.

The Gospel of John, with its portraits of Jesus in the "I am" texts, is an inspiration for the Sethian *Acts of John*. Jesus leads the choir in *The Round Dance of the Soul* and a Chorus responds during the dance: Jesus says, "The whole universe takes part in dancing." The circling chorus responds:

> Amen. I have no house and I have houses./I have no temple and I have temples./I am a lamp to you who see me./I am a mirror to you who perceive me./I am a door to you who knock on me./I am a way to you, you passerby. Amen.[21]

Meyer refers to John the Baptist in another gnostic text, *The Secret Book of James*, which was unearthed with the Nag Hammadi scrolls.[22] John the Baptizer's death by beheading is cryptically recalled in a conversation that Jesus has with his disciples. The apostle James inquires about one's ability to prophesy. Jesus answers,

> "Do you not know that the head of prophecy was cut off with John?" But I said, "Master, is it not impossible to remove the head of prophecy?" The master said to me, "When you realize what 'head' means, and that prophecy comes from the head, then understand the meaning of 'its head was removed.'"[23]

John's head is entombed in Damascus's central mosque, formerly the basilica dedicated to St. John (*Yahya* in Arabic; see Appendix B). The Qur'an honors John as a prophet when his name appears on a list of eighteen other biblical prophets.[24] A Sethian document translated by Marvin Meyer, *The Second Treatise of the Great Seth*, asserts that Jesus' death was a hoax. This treatise refers to Adam, but not Seth, as a laughingstock because Adam became a lackey to the evil ruler of this world, Ialdabaoth. Others accused of being a laughingstock include Abraham, Isaac, Jacob, Moses, David, Solomon (because he thought he was Christ), and John the Baptist for not recognizing the hidden Christ, a constant theme in gnostic writings, and also Simon of Cyrene who was crucified rather than Jesus. The "laughing," true emanation of Jesus proclaims:

> For my death, which they think happened, happened to them in their error and blindness, since they nailed their man unto their death. Their thoughts did not see me, for they were deaf and

---

21. Barnstone and Meyer, *Gnostic Bible*, 353–54.
22. Barnstone and Meyer, *Gnostic Bible*, 340.
23. Barnstone and Meyer, *Gnostic Bible*, 345.
24. Ali, *Meaning of the Holy Qur'an*, 6:84–85, 317.

blind... It was another, their father, who drank the gall and the vinegar; it was not I. They struck me with the reed; it was another, Simon, who bore the cross on his shoulder. It was another upon whom they placed the crown of thorns. But I was rejoicing in the height over all the wealth of the rulers and the offspring of their error, of their empty glory. And I was laughing at their ignorance.[25]

Once the Christian churches formed their alliances for and against Triune creeds during their first five centuries, the gnostics were banished to desert caves and isolated monasteries. However, by the end of the millennium, the gospel narratives of Jesus' death on the cross were once again challenged when the Arab and Islamic forces moved out of the desert into the Christian heartlands of Egypt, Syria, and Mesopotamia. The Qur'an would deny the crucifixion of the Messiah, Jesus.[26] An empty tomb in Medina next to the prophet Muhammad's tomb is waiting for Jesus to return to earth where he'll live out his life and die a natural death (see Appendix B).

---

25. Barnstone and Meyer, *Gnostic Bible*, 469–70.
26. Qur'an 4:157, 237.

6

Saints of the Orthodox East

Icons and Iconoclasts

SYRIA, HER CAPITAL, DAMASCUS, and her various Syriac languages proclaimed a vibrant Christian presence starting with St. Paul's Damascus Road conversion and his Antiochian disciples being offhandedly named Christians.[1] Antioch was third in size in the Roman Empire, after Rome and Alexandria, and the place where two or perhaps all of the four Gospels were first read. Syrian Christianity grew with a steady stream of conversions, giving rise to conflicts with their Byzantine overlords. A period of massive expansion under the Muslim Umayyad Caliphate ended by AD 750 and the Arab-Islamic capital moved from Damascus to a new capital on the banks of the Tigris River. Syriac dialects, icons, and monks kept Christianity alive at the popular level, and future saints sought healing for the divisions within Orthodox Christianity. Today, Syrian saints' icons are adored throughout the modern world, and in South India, Syriac is still used in the liturgies of the Mar Thoma Church.

Origen, an Egyptian born in Alexandria in AD 185, is viewed by many as the founder of Christian scholarship. Third-century church historian and bishop, Eusebius, recalled how Origen mastered several Hebrew texts during a lifetime of teaching, often narrowly escaping death.[2] After his father's martyrdom, Origen traveled to Rome where severe persecution had taken the lives of many of Jesus' followers. His instructions for bishops and other church leaders in Jerusalem, Arabia, and Antioch emphasized the

---

1. Acts 11:26 RSV.
2. Eusebius, *History of the Church*, 256.

incarnation of Jesus, the Christ, in the Logos of John's Gospel who "tabernacled" among his believers.³

Origen died under arrest and in ill health during the rule of Caesar Decius (AD 249–251).

Fig. 47—Emperor Decius, Goddess Tyche Coin

This Roman gold coin bears the human image of the emperor who is designated god in the Latin inscription in the border surrounding Decius' laurel-crowned head. On the reverse side, the city goddess, Tyche, holds the sacred caduceus with a single coiled serpent. The caduceus symbols are not so frightening today as two snakes climbing a pole are stitched on jackets worn by medical, pharmaceutical, and other health servers.

Latin and Greek words describe the whole engraving process as *kharactar* and for Decius his character role as the deified Caesar was *Felicitas*, happiness and prosperity; a far cry from his three-year reign mainly fighting on Rome's northern frontier where he died along with his son. Theologians were inspired by the subject of the God-Man, Jesus, who is introduced in the book of Hebrews as one who *reflects the very stamp (kharactar) of God's nature*.⁴ Harold Brown credits Origen for advocating Jesus' *character* as stamped God and Man, the Incarnate One.⁵ The inscribed name for Decius, *Felicitas*, is an example of the rigid human attributes in contrast to the familial name, Son, which resonates throughout the book of Hebrews.

Among the individuals who rose to prominence in the Syrian region of Rome's provinces are a Roman Emperor, Philip I, two well-documented

---

3. John 1:14 RSV.

4. Hebrews 1:3 RSV.

5. Brown, *Heresies*, 89.

and acclaimed saints, Ephrem and John of Damascus, and a pseudo-disciple of Paul who nevertheless was found to be worthy of a saints' day on October 9. Caesar Philip I presided over the 1,000-year celebration of the founding of Rome (AD 247–248) a year before he and his son, Philip II, were killed in a revolt by one of Philip's own generals, Decius, who would succeed him as Caesar. Decius' short rule ended in AD 251. The goddess Tyche's coin images symbolize Imperial Rome granting limited freedom to the Greek and other conquered provinces. Tyche will endure for generations as a Miss Liberty figurehead.

Fig. 48—Caesar Philip, Goddess Tyche Coin

Philip's rise to Caesarian status came through the equestrian ranks, but his Arab background from the lowly eastern borderlands was a bias that Philip could not overcome. Historian G. W. Bowersock reserves his opinion on Philip being a Christian, but says that Decius resumed the persecution of Christians after Philip's death.[6] Following several uprisings in the Roman world, Emperor Diocletian divided the empire into Eastern and Western locations and then led one of the most ruthless persecutions against Christians before abdicating in AD 305. After several claimants to the throne were defeated, Constantine the Great was proclaimed emperor by his troops in York, England, whom he rallied in the year AD 312, conquering a rival to his throne in the battle of Milvian Bridge near Rome. A vision of *Chi Rho*, "Conquer by this," opened new vistas for Christians and a new capital for Constantine at the crossroads of Europe and Asia. Once established in Byzantium and renamed Constantinople (Arabicized *Istambul*), Constantine issued edicts of toleration for Christians, built churches, and

---

6. Bowersock, *Roman Arabia*, 123.

promoted church unity. In a commemorative coin minted after his death, Constantine rides in a chariot emblematic of his heavenly entry while the outstretched hand of God welcomes him.

Fig. 49—Byzantine Hand of God Coin

Constantine summoned the Ecumenical Council to settle the nature of the divine Logos—theological concerns of God as Father and God's relationship to the only begotten Son. The results from the stormy gatherings eventually became the Nicene Creed, a Trinitarian statement which Constantine endorsed after the opposing bishops insisted on words emphasizing that the incarnation proclaims that Jesus Christ was not only truly God, but also truly man. The Syrian churches accepted the Chalcedonian Ecumenical Creed in AD 451 when the weighty doctrinal debates on the divinity of Christ seemed to be settled. Later the Syrian Christians were joined by Egyptians and Ethiopians in recognizing that Christ's humanity was transformed to become one divine nature, or monophysitism. Growing out of this controversy was the split of the Roman Church from the Eastern Orthodox Church and then the Eastern Churches subdivided over monophysitism under the name of a heretical bishop, Nestorius. Brown notes the Nestorians and the monophysites, unlike the gnostics, were firmly within the bounds of the Nicene creedal orthodoxy.[7]

A mixed media for the fourth Christian century could not have a better model than the theologian-poet Ephrem the Syrian, who proclaimed the Orthodox message in the Syriac tongue, combining the biblical and theological topics into verses of poetry and hymns.

---

7. Brown, *Heresies*, 159.

Fig. 50—Icon of St. Ephrem

The future saint was born in Nisibis when it was under Roman rule, but following the defeat of the Byzantines by the Sasanians, he moved westward to Edessa where he spent most of his life in what his biographer Brock called "proto-monasticism."[8] St. Ephrem's famed maxim, "He gave us divinity, we gave him humanity," celebrates the mystery of the incarnation.[9] Human eyes and ears extol not only the Creator, but also the creature:

> Scriptures refers to His 'ears,' to teach us that He listens to us; it speaks of. His 'eyes,' to show that He sees us. . . He put on these names too because of our weakness.[10]

The names, "The All Hearer" and "The All Seeing" will reappear in the Qur'an and in the 99 names, echoing the auspicious poetry of Ephrem.

8. Brock, *Luminous Eye*, 17.
9. Brock, *Luminous Eye*, 154.
10. Brock, *Luminous Eye*, 60.

His images are articulate commentaries on the names of God rather than standard adjectival attributes. Ephrem invites his congregants to a feast that includes a metaphorical descent into the Christian rite of baptism. The Wedding Feast at Cana is one of praise and Jesus is the special guest.[11]

A non-Syrian contemporary of St. Ephrem was St. Gregory of Nazianzen who came from Cappadocia, the Greek-speaking region in Asia Minor. Gregory was a skillful theologian and poet like Ephrem, and both solemnized the divine creation of humanity. According to Gregory, Adam's creation out of dusty earth was beamed from celestial radiance:

> The soul is a breath of God, and though heavenly, it allows itself to mingle with the earth. It is the light shut up in a cave, but is none the less a light divine and inextinguishable.[12]

Gregory, his elder brother St. Basil, and another Gregory (of Nyssa) were acclaimed as Trinitarian defenders, along with the Egyptian St. Athanasius, during the fourth century when there were pockets of opposition to the creed. An Arabian sect, El Kesaite, not only troubled Origen and Bishop Eusebius, but left impressions upon the young Mani several centuries later.[13] Orthodox theologian Lossky praises the gospel writers St. John the Evangelist, and Gregory Nazianzen, for their contributions to Syrian mysticism which exposed Gnosticism as "knowledge for its own sake." The ultimate triumph of Christian theology in the Syriac and Greek fathers is the mystical union with God, according to Lossky.[14] This union begins at creation with the presence of the Holy Spirit, who is the one in the Trinity that Nazianzen highlights in his dogma of the Spirit, which is summarized by Lossky:

> The Old Testament manifested the Father plainly, the Son obscurely. The New Testament revealed the Son and hinted at the divinity of the Holy Spirit. Today the Spirit dwells among us and makes Him more clearly known.[15]

The Holy Spirit is the one making Christ known, but humankind is incapable of knowing all there is to know about the Ineffable One. The monastic, ascetic faith soon was wrapped in a system of theology called Negative or Apophatic. This was embraced by Eastern Christians while Western

---

11. Brock, *Luminous Eye*, 124–25.
12. Lossky, *Mystical Theology*, 117.
13. Eusebius, *History of the Church*, 272.
14. Lossky, *Mystical Theology*, 9.
15. Lossky, *Mystical Theology*, 161.

Christians, according to the Russian Orthodox Lossky, were less inclined to break with their classical Hellenistic thoughts on Unity so as to subscribe to inscrutable, even contradictory, notations on the Trinity.[16]

Dionysius first introduced himself as a Greek from Athens who was a convert of Paul and his disciple, Timothy, after the apostle preached in the local Areopagus plaza (Acts 17:22–34). He left a small body of treatises and letters which offered much about his theological genius, but little personal information, yet his apostolic veracity continued to be accepted for over 500 years by both the Latin (Roman) and Eastern Churches as Dionysius the Areopagite, the first bishop of Athens. In an introduction by Jaroslav Pelikan to *Pseudo-Dionysius: The Complete Works*, an earlier interpretation of Dionysius as a Monophysite Patriarch of Antioch during the fifth or sixth centuries is dismissed.[17] Pelikan mentions that Dionysius was quoted by Thomas Aquinas about 1,700 times.[18] European Reformers were eager to expose Dionysius as an imposter to bolster their Protestant causes against papal infallibility, which was a prominent topic of one of the Dionysius treatises. Dionysius' *The Divine Names* was the largest of Dionysius' texts translated by Luibheid and opens with a discourse on the transcendence of God manifested by the following names: "God," "Lord of Lords," "God of Gods," "King of Kings," "Name above every name," "Cause of the ages," "greatest of all and yet the one in the still breeze."[19] The breeze which Elijah heard (1 Kgs 19:11–12) wafted on Dionysius' ears: God is praised in Scripture as "great," as in greatness, and the "still small breeze which reveals the divine smallness."[20] "Small" is the opposite of "great" yet singly or together conveyed God's character. The name Ancient of Days (Dan 7:9, 13, 22) presented the Almighty in eternity, beyond time, but also in a very limited period of time: days.[21] God's transcendence was illuminated in St. Paul's letter to the Philippians where he extols the name of Jesus as "a name above every name."[22] Dionysius' divine names proclaims the nameless, Transcendent One as an appositive to the named One, Goodness.[23] In

---

16. Lossky, *Mystical Theology*, 49, 50.
17. Dionysius, *Pseudo-Dionysius*, 13.
18. Dionysius, *Pseudo-Dionysius*, 21.
19. Dionysius, *Pseudo-Dionysius*, 55.
20. Dionysius, *Pseudo-Dionysius*, 115.
21. Dionysius, *Pseudo-Dionysius*, 120–21.
22. Phil 2:9 RSV.
23. Dionysius, *Pseudo-Dionysius*, 54.

his essay on angels, Dionysius advocated a heavenly hierarchy based upon the mystery of Jesus' birth in the presence of the angels and shepherds. The high immanence as announced by angels also declares that Jesus never did abandon that human form which he chose and obediently submitted to please God the Father.[24]

The Dionysian divine names served as a prelude to a much shorter treatise called *The Mystical Theology* that transcended the theology of the very names he was extolling in the original essay. St. Gregory Nazianzen mentions how Jesus' disciples followed the Savior to the Mount of Transfiguration (Mt. Tabor), which was analogous to Dionysius' urgings for Christians to ascend with Moses on Mt. Sinai and to climb beyond reason to approach God in silence. Dionysius' mystical prayer opens *Mystical Theology*:

> Lead us up beyond unknowing and light,/up to the farthest, highest peak/of mystic scripture,/where the mysteries of God's Word/ lie simple, absolute and unchangeable/in the brilliant darkness of a hidden silence./Amid the deepest shadow/they pour overwhelming light/on what is most manifest.[25]

John of Damascus is one of the most honored theologians of the universal church, joining Dionysius, Gregory, and Ephrem as theologian-poets who knew the power of language, as well as images that nourish the souls of Christians. The most recognizable among his words in English is John's resurrection hymn:

> Come, ye faithful, raise the strain/of triumphant gladness:/God hath brought His people forth/Into joy from sadness/Now rejoice, Jerusalem,/And with true affection/Welcome in unwearied strains/Jesus' resurrection.[26]

---

24. Dionysius, *Pseudo-Dionysius*, 158.
25. Dionysius, *Pseudo-Dionysius*, 135.
26. Damascene, "Day of Resurrection," 151.

Fig. 51—Icon of John of Damascus

His personal story is legendary, a life augmented by saintly hagiographical legends. A visitor to the Mar Saba monastery ten miles southeast of Jerusalem will confront a large painting of John inside the cave where he did much of his sacred writing. John's right hand is marked at the wrist by a scarred line. According to the legend reported in Schaff's history, the hand was severed by an Umayyad caliph after his loyal subject, a trusted treasurer in the Arab court, was charged with forgery. John prayed to the Virgin Mary and his hand returned to the wrist.[27] Muslims, Saracens, *without Sarah*, or Ishmaelites, were less trouble than the disagreement over icons within his

27. Schaff, *History of the Christian Church*, 4:628.

Byzantine Orthodox Church. John defended the veneration of icons in the churches against the edicts of the emperor, patriarchs, and bishops committed to Constantinople. The imperial position known as iconoclasm provoked the following anathemas against John by disparaging his Arabic Syrian name, Mansur, and cited here by John's biographer, Andrew Louth:

> To Mansur, the one with a vile-sounding name and of Saracen opinion, anathema!/To the worshipper of icons and writer of falsehoods, Mansur, anathema!/To the insulter of Christ and conspirator against the Empire, Mansur, anathema.[28]

The caliphate protection of John from these curses was an expression of appreciation for the skills and loyalty that he and his immediate forebears offered the Umayyads. John's father was treasurer for the caliph, an esteemed position close to what John would occupy. The grandfather was either praised or condemned for opening the gates of Damascus when the Muslims conquered the city. The surrender was partly a survival tactic and partly out of abhorrence of the Greeks, years before the ban on icons in AD 624. Caliph Abd al-Malik began to reform the Greek-Christian currency to Arab-Muslim currency in the Hijra years (77–80 AH, also known as the Islamic calendar) when the off-the-desert Arabs were still expanding and depending on former civil administrators to manage their empire. Before the completion of new mints, Arab-Byzantine coins were available in Syrian areas and Arab-Sasanian coins were used in former Sasanian provinces.

Fig. 52—Byzantine-Arab Bronze Coin

---

28. Louth, *St. John Damascene*, 197.

Historian Louth links Dionysius and John together in an apophatic theology that stresses negation of all theologies because whatever one proposes regarding God, that too must be transcended.[29]

Christians in the Eastern churches who once composed the majority of the population gradually diminished to become minorities that fractured further into denominations that matched political divisions. For instance, Jacobites and Melkites were largely located in Syrian provinces, while the Nestorians, renamed Assyrians and later Chaldeans, established their homelands in what is modern Iraq. In the northern mountain highlands these two Arab nations juxtaposed with Turks from Central Asia and Persian-speaking Iranians, and where the pacified Christians obeyed the authorities according to Romans 13. While the Christian state of Georgia on the border of these Sasanian/Islamic states had Russia as a protective power, the Armenians were embedded among the majority religions and often surrendered territories and rights to the Persians and Arabs.

Fig. 53—Armenian Church

---

29. Louth, *St. John Damascene*, 223.

At the end of the eighth century the Church of the East, with her Nestorian Patriarch, moved from Ctesiphon, the Sasanian capital, to the Abbasid capital, Baghdad. The Christians, as well as Jews, were granted some local parochial rule. John Joseph reports that the system of government meant that Jews and Christians as "People of the Book" were protected, but without equality in citizenship.

> [N]on-Muslim sects were put under the jurisdiction of the religious heads of their respective creeds . . . whose jurisdiction extended to matters of personal status, such as marriage and inheritance, but also most of the disputes among the community.[30]

Paying the annual poll tax, the *Jizyah*, was assessed as a gold dinar and served as a military exemption fee for non-Muslims males. Rabbis, as well as monks, priests, and bishops, literally held in their hands the well-being and the security of their parishioners when they applied their seals on documents dealing with birth to death and other family affairs.

Fig. 54—Church Seal of Limited Authority

The seal has markers at both ends of this cylinder, a cross on the narrow end, and illegible markings at the broad end. Christians were allowed to privately record deaths on their gravestones which were often desecrated during times of disturbances.

---

30. Joseph, *Nestorians and Muslims Neighbors*, 27.

Fig. 55—Tombstone of Christian

The first written Arabic is on a Nabatean Christian tombstone on Mt. Nebo in Jordan (see Appendix B).

Nestorians left many epitaphs in Mongolian and Chinese languages at the eastern terminus of the Silk Road. Under Arab and Persian authority, Christians were unable to propagate their faith in their homelands, but monks and lay missionaries travelled freely to Asia and established many congregations.

7

Zoroaster and Ahuramazda

This Zarathustra Spoke

The blogger *monkeymind* presents the case for Zoroaster as the first monotheist whose origins are from 1000 BC. However, James Ford grants that the monotheism of Pharaoh Akhenaton (d. 1353) would be older (see Fig. 04). He refers to the Hebrew Bible's account of the Babylonian captivity without mentioning the earlier biblical records of Patriarchs Abraham and Moses, who lived before the tenth century.[1] The seventy years of Jewish exile in Babylon beginning with the destruction of Jerusalem in 586 BC allows some claims that Zoroastrianism and its god, Ahuramazda, did move the religion of the Jews from a tribal polytheism, a my-god-is-better-than-your-gods belief, to true monotheism for the Jews in Babylon. Daniel, the book and the person, demonstrates that the Old Testament monotheism was alive for a faithful remnant of the Hebrew-speaking people before and after the Babylon captivity.

Fig. 56—Zoroaster, Modern Sketch

1. http://patheos.com/monkeymind/author/jamesford.

ZOROASTER AND AHURAMAZDA

The prophet Zarathustra, here designated Zoroaster, and Ahuramazda, often written Ahura Mazda, were worshipped by millions for two millennia. Ford notes that currently the believers are reduced to two and half million, primarily in India, where they are known as Parsees and their faith called Mazadaism. The wings of Ahuramazda allegedly became more than a symbol for the Jews when angels appeared in Daniel and in other Hebrew Scriptures. Also, the Zoroastrian contacts during exile years contributed to the beliefs in resurrection and judgments as heralded by the archangel Michael in the book of Daniel:

> At that time shall arise Michael, the great prince who has charge of your people. And there shall be a time of trouble, such as never has been since there was a nation till that time; but at that time your people will be delivered, every one whose name shall be found written in the book. And many of those who sleep in the dust of the earth shall awake, some to everlasting life, and some to shame and everlasting contempt.[2]

The subject of the afterlife leads to the resurrection of Jesus Christ as an essential *kerygma* of the Gospels and Paul's Epistles. A scholar of the previous century, James Moulton, suggests there are reasons for this other than a direct one-way Jewish absorption of Avesta Scriptures and practices.[3] Moulton provides a list of divine names extracted from various editions of the Avesta, the Zoroastrian Scriptures. Neither the name Resurrector, nor any other analogous references to after-death existences, were among three lists totaling over seventy-five sacred names.[4] Ahuramazda's attributes include Creator, Protector, Knower, Wise, and several other common divine names. But Herd-giver and Word of the Cattle Owner are reflections of an agricultural society related to Indian and Iranian cowmen. Mary Boyce's volumes on Zoroastrianism connect the earliest followers of the prophet Zarathustra to the Indian Buddhist emperor Aśoka from readings on the Thirteenth Rock inscriptions[5] (see Fig. 06). Boyce mentions that Aśoka's *Dhamma* directed Zoroastrians toward peace and religious tolerance.[6] Zoroaster, once considered the master of the magi,[7] was active in the Scythian

---

2. Dan 12:1–2 RSV.
3. Moulton, *Treasure of the Magi*, 72–73.
4. Moulton, *Treasure of the Magi*, 95–96.
5. Boyce, *History of Zoroastrianism*, 3:146.
6. Boyce, *History of Zoroastrianism*, 3:141.
7. Boyce, *History of Zoroastrianism*, 3:368.

and Median empires and during the Parthian period at the close of the first millennium. The magi, an inherited priestly class, were more active within the Zoroastrian-dominated monarchies, as well as the Achaemenian and Sasanian dynasties, which were centered in Persia. Cyrus, the Achaemenian emperor, surrounded himself with *haddaberin* (counselors) whom Daniel refers to by this exclusive Persian title (Dan 3:24, 4:36, 6:7).

Cyrus decreed that the Jews be allowed to return to Jerusalem after their seventy-year exile (2 Chr 36:22–23). The Judean scribe Ezra, writing in Hebrew and Aramaic, mentions that Cyrus ordered the return of temple vessels and as the king of kings he received reports about the rebuilding of the walls and temple of Jerusalem (Ezra 1–2). Cyrus' more honorific titles occur in the book of Isaiah where the Persian king is identified as a shepherd (Isa 44:28) and as a messianic, divinely anointed figure (Isa 45:1). Anointing kings and priests presumes holy rites, but olive oil smeared on the heads of sheep to ward off insects (Ps 23:5) suggests humbler uses. Smearing oil on wounds or heads of state in Hebrew is *mashiah,* translated into Greek as *Christos.* Paul, a Jewish follower of Jesus, the Christ, the Anointed, reminded the gentile believers that they were metaphorically a wild olive branch grafted into a cultivated olive tree, a symbol of Judaism (Rom 11:24). The pressed olive berry produces oil for the anointing of foods and the heads of kings and priests. Cyrus' conquests extended Persia's borders west to Greek areas of Asia Minor and to Central Asian Bactria on the east. After his defeat of the Babylonians and the return of over 40,000 Jews to Jerusalem, Cyrus died on a battlefield and is buried in Pasargadae where magi priests guarded the tomb for a couple of centuries (see Appendix B). His successor, Darius, pushed the imperial borders into Greece, Egypt, and deeper into southwest Asia. The governors, *satraps,* stayed in touch with each other through a network that is recycled into the motto of the US Postal System's pledge of service ("Through rain, through snow, through hail...") where the messengers, saddled heralds, were able to make their stations covering over 1,600 miles in a week. Cyrus and Darius issued edicts recognizing their devotion to Ahuramazda. Both emperors are memorialized by inscriptions carved into a cliff at Naqsh-i-Rustam in central Iran. A translation of the code of Darius became available in English in the nineteenth century:

> A great God is Ahuramazda, who created this earth, who created yonder sky, who created happiness for man, who made Darius King, one king of many, one lord of many. I am Darius, the great king, king of kings, king of countries containing all kinds of men, king in

this great earth far and wide, son of Hystaspes, an Achaemenian, a Persian, son of a Persian, and Aryan, having a Aryan lineage. King Darius says: By the favor of Ahuramazda these are the countries which I seized outside of Persia; I ruled over them; they bore tribute to me; what was to them by me that they did; my law—that they held them firm. . . Scythians with pointed caps, Babylonia, Assyria, Arabia, Armenia, Cappadocia, Sardis, Ionia, Scythians who are across the sea, (Saka), Petasos-wearing Greeks (Yauna), the Libyans, the Ethiopians, the men of Maka and the Carians. . . O man, that which is the command of Ahuramazda, let this not seem repugnant to you; do not leave the right path; do not rise in rebellion! [8]

The Achaemenid period ended with Alexander transmitting a veneer of Greek culture to the former Persian Empire and into Egypt and the Indus Valleys. Alexander mistook all of Zoroaster's followers for *Magoi*, a confusion that endured long after the fall of the Persian nation. The magi were not participants in the mass wedding of Alexander's noblemen warriors with Persian women in Susa.[9] Seleucus, Alexander's general, was one of more than eighty grooms, along with Alexander and some 1,000 other Macedonian soldiers, who were given wedding gifts. The Seleucid Empire did keep the Greek language alive on official edicts and coins, while Aramaic languages were spoken by the masses, including Jesus of Nazareth. Seleucus Nicator, the former general, is profiled on a silver *tetradrachm* coin in a natural middle age pose without the pagan gods' trappings of lion's heads and horns that were on Alexander's coins (see Fig. 17) On the reverse of this coin, Athena is short-shirted, if not shortchanged, with a shield and anchor, standing in a chariot pulled by four-horned elephants.

Fig. 57—Seleucus Nicator Coin

8. Talman, *Guide to the Old Persian Inscriptions*, 146.
9. Cartledge, *Alexander the Great*, 105.

The decline of worship of Ahuramazda did not harm the magi, who adapted to the changing times. During the rule of one of the last Parthian kings, a group of magi pondered over their astrological charts following the eclipse of the planet Jupiter on April 17, 6 BC, conjecturing that this signified the presence of a new and important ruler. Would these curious magi leave the safety of the Parthian capital, likely Ctesiphon, and risk searching for a new-born king in Judah?

In the opening years of the second century AD, another Iranian-based empire appeared and continued without interruption to AD 651, when finally the last of twenty-nine Sasanian monarchs became a casualty of his own people in the midst of Arab military campaigns for Islam. Shapur II began his seventy-year reign in AD 309, the year after Mani began his mission. Shapur was convinced by the magi that Mani was a traitor, and subsequently the latter was crucified. Initially, Shapur tolerated a sizeable peaceful Christian presence inside Persia, but his western border was constantly tested by Byzantine forces and the Christian nation of Armenia. These wars embittered him against the Christian subjects within his territories and persecution ensued. Today in the city of Susa, biblical name Shushan (Esth 1:5), is the rebuilt tomb for the prophet Daniel that serves as a reminder for visitors of a great history now spread over a large archaeological wilderness. Shapur II destroyed much of the city, along with a great cathedral, in retaliation for border losses.[10] Sasanian coins function as reminders of the weighty crowns on the heads of kings and queens who appear on the obverse, while the coin's reverse depicts a flaming altar of three steps guarded by two attending magi.

Fig. 58—Shapur II, Altar Coin

10. Matheson, *Persia*, 148, 150.

ZOROASTER AND AHURAMAZDA

Another strong leader, Khusro II, was the local hero for capturing the true cross relic, but a villain for Jerusalem Christians after sacking the whole Palestinian region, destroying churches and monasteries. The Hepthalites, an obscure tribe, often identified as Huns, would chip away at the Persian's eastern borders. Emperor Khusro II's silver *drachma* has a Hepthalite scorpion-punched mark on his coin. Khusro II was assassinated by his own people and two years later his daughter, Buran, returned the cross to the Byzantine emperors, Heraclius and his son.

Fig. 59—Khusro II Punched-Mark Coin

Once the Arab forces began their attacks on both the Byzantine and Sasanian empires, the mints of the vanquished nations were put out of service. For instance, the coins of Khusro I (d. 579 AD) remained in circulation long after the Arab conquests. The Arabs imitated the abundant and widely recognized *drachms* of Khusro II, but added "in the name of Allah" or "to Allah" on the borders of coins. They did not, however, strike imitative *drachms* for Queen Buran, daughter of Khusro II. She was queen for just over one year and produced very few coins, hence her image was not nearly as familiar.

Fig. 60—Queen Buran Sasanian Coin

The two competing empires—Greek-*Rum* vs. *Persian*-Sasanian—weakened by centuries of costly rivalries, left the door open for the Arabs' response to the prophet Muhammad's call to restore a simpler faith in the One God, Allah. Captive Persian artisans' handiwork is embedded in mosaics that adorn the walls and ceilings of the Dome of the Rock in Jerusalem. This mosaic copies the design of the crown worn by Khusro II.

Fig. 61—Persian Mosaics in the Dome of the Rock

8

Muhammad, Prophet of Allah

The Qur'an Speaks Arabic

MONKS TREKKED WITH CARAVANS or lingered in monastic cave cells scattered along the Gazan Mediterranean coast, extending south to Hadramawt near the tip of the Arabian Peninsula, where gold, frankincense, and myrrh were traded long before the days of Augustus Caesar. Midway down this desert landmass between Roman and Sasanian empires were located the two oasis towns of Mecca and Medina. Jews and Christians lived amid a polytheistic Arab population which included Muhammad, who fled his birth city, Mecca, for Medina in AD 622, year one of Hijra on the Islamic calendar (AH). Because Mecca depended heavily on the Arab tribal pilgrimages to the Black Stone, a meteorite inside the Ka'ba, Muhammad was ostracized and threatened with death when his revelations led him to oppose the Meccan pagan rites.

Fig. 62—Mecca Black Stone, Ka'ba

He was not alone during the Meccan years as his distant cousin, the monk Waraqa Ibn Nawfal, and a small group of followers of the prophet Abraham, stood with him against their tribal kinsmen. Waraqa belonged to a Christian-Jewish sect and translated selections from the Gospel of Matthew into Arabic while affirming the prophet Muhammad's revelations that he received in a Mt. Hira cave outside of Mecca. When Waraqa died in AD 619, the revelations ceased, but resumed later in Medina. The Qur'an calls for the worship of the One God, Allah, yet the two monotheistic faiths opposed the nascent Muslim community. In Medina, a sizeable Jewish community rejected Muhammad's prophethood and his interpretations of previous Scriptures. Arabic-speaking Christians rejected the Qur'an's message that Jesus the Messiah, was not the divine son of God. The prophet died in AD 633 in Medina where his tomb is a mosque (see Appendix B).

The Qur'anic revelations that came down (*nazala*) spoke to the prophet's off-the-record inquiries from his own nonmonotheistic Arab tribesmen who were considered "illiterate" (*ummi*), without an Arab prophet. This stood in contrast to the prophets who spoke through their writings to the Jews and the *Nasara*, the name for Christians in the Qur'an. Miraculously, Arabic was the language Allah spoke to answer Muhammad's inquiries. The Qur'an mentions the "ease" of knowing the Arabic language in comprehending the renewal and recertification of the former messages, the Torah and the gospel, *Injil*, thereby correcting the stories about Moses and Jesus the Messiah. "Verily, We have made this (Qur'an) easy in thy tongue, in order that they may give heed."[1]

The answers to Muhammad's questions often begin with the exhortation, "Remember" with reference to previous revelations, some from the Bible, but several from sources outside of the Hebrew and Greek Scriptures. The longest surah in the Qur'an, the second, "The Calf," asks Moses to remember the golden calf (*al-Baqarah*) that his people worshipped while he was receiving the Law on Mt. Sinai.[2] Surah 38:22–26 tells the story of David listening to a shepherd who has one ewe stolen by his brother who had ninety-nine ewes. David makes the wise decision and the shepherd's brother falls down and asks forgiveness. In the Bible narrative, King David is confronted by the prophet Nathan and the dispute ends with the king asking forgiveness (2 Sam 12:7–15). In the Qur'an, the dispute ends with a tribute to David making him vicegerent: (Caliph) "O David! We did indeed

---

1. Qur'an, 44:58, 1291.
2. Qur'an 2:53–54, 29, 30.

make thee a vicegerent on earth: so judge thou between men in truth."³ The modern Israeli coin shows David wearing a religious headpiece.

Fig. 63—King David, Israeli Coin

When Christians and Jews read the Qur'an, the non-Muslims tend to treat the stories as borrowed from previous Scriptures and embellished by Muhammad for his Arabic-speaking community. An example of the Qur'an's nonbiblical source is the long narrative about Moses when he is on a journey and he meets the Dhu al Qarnayn (Surah 18:60), the two-horned character first introduced in Daniel 8:6, and found on Alexander's coin (see Fig. 17). Parenthetically, Moses is artfully embellished with the two horns in Michelangelo's famous sculpture which is based upon St. Jerome's fourth-century mistaken translation in the Latin Vulgate Bible of Exodus 34:29. Moses descends from Mt. Sinai with horns rather than the *splendor* on his face.

---

3. Qur'an 38:26, 1166.

Fig. 64—Michelangelo's Moses with Horns

Also, Surah 18, the Sleepers of the Cave,[4] relates a Christian legend that had been embellished by centuries of constant retelling. Medical doctor Khaled Sanadiki remarks on the reverberating effects of the story of the seven Christian youth:

> . . . was translated into many languages, including Ethiopian, Coptic and Arabic. The story moved west and found its way into Byzantine literature. . . and was eventually translated into Latin, where it was copied and recounted through the ages, and is found in Anglo-Saxon, Medieval German, ancient Norse, Swedish, Italian, French and Spanish literature.[5]

The Qur'an mentions a dated coin of Caesar Decius (see Fig. 47) and the sleeping dog, adding to the mystical ambience of these seven Ephesian youths whose sleeping images appear in diverse religious art forms. The icon here owned by the Russian Bezayiff family does not show the dog or the coin.

---

4. Qur'an 18:9–26, 709–716.
5. Sanadiki, *Legends & Narratives*, 289.

Fig. 65—Seven Sleepers Icon

The Qur'an affirms this Christian legend in Surah 18, titled "The Cave," when the awakened sleepers confess the unadulterated belief of Islamic monotheism (verses 14 and 15). The Ephesian lads discuss the unknown length of time that they were sleeping in the cave when a coin is produced that will supply a clue.[6]

---

6. Qur'an 18:19, 712–713. Caesar Decius is identified in Footnote 2337, 709 of the Qur'an.

On the coin's face is Decius who was Caesar from 249 to 251 AD during a reign of severe persecution of Christians. The one delegated to go to town to buy bread with the scripted coin would expect similar persecution. However, rather than persecution, the seven discovered that their Christian faith had turned into a non-Unitarian, a Trinitarian creed. Islam rejects the divine Sonship but endorses the pre-Nicene (325 AD) Christian message recognized by these seven sleepers.

Jesus' parable of the sower, along with allegorical embellishment, is found with slight modifications in the first three Gospels. Mark's Gospel records a shorter parable of four verses that emphasizes the unobservable growth and the judgment at the harvest.

> "The kingdom of God is as if a man should scatter seed upon the ground, and should sleep and rise night and day, and the seed should sprout and grow, he knows not how. The earth produces of itself, first the blade, then the ear, then full grain in the ear. But when the grain is ripe, at once he puts in the sickle, because the harvest has come."[7]

The Qur'an defines the three stages of growth in a rare instance of using biblical words such as *mithal* (Hebrew parable), *euengelia* (Greek-Aramaic gospel), and *zer'a* (Hebrew seed):

> This is their similitude (*mithlu*) in the Tawrah; and their similitude in the Gospel (*al-Injil*) is like a seed (*zer'a*) which sends forth its blade, then makes it strong; it then becomes thick, and stands on its own stem, (filling) the sowers with wonder. As a result, it fills the Unbelievers with rage at them.[8]

The Qur'an's interpretation of the three stages of the wheat's growth parallels the three stages of the Abrahamic faiths, stating that the first two revelations/books, Torah and gospel (blade and stem), have reached their growth, but the fruit of the seed is Islam. Jews and Christians will be provoked to jealousy as Islam becomes the fruit at harvest time. The amazing growth of Islam was displayed in its overpowering of two empires, the Byzantine and Sasanian. Coins will partially tell the stories of the defeated empires such as the Sasanian coin of Khusro II remaining in circulation during the long Arab rule (see Fig. 59). However, in the former Byzantine realms, John of Damascus' loyal service for the ambitious Abd al-Malik

---

7. Mark 4:26–29 RSV.
8. Qur'an 48:29, 1337.

strengthened the Umayyad Empire through the power of the mints (see Fig. 51). Reference to the sower parable is found on this AD 1304 coin of a celebrated convert to Islam named Uljaytu, who changed his Mongol name to Khudabanda when he adopted Shi'a Islam. The coin also lists the Twelve Shi'a Imams.

Fig. 66—Uljaytu 'Sower' Dinar Coin

On all Arabic coins the following phrase appears: "There is no god but Allah and Muhammad is the messenger of God." This creed, known as the *Kalima (word)*, has been stamped on Islamic coins since Abd al-Malik, the fifth Umayyad Caliph in 83 AH. "No god but God" is on the obverse center, with the name and date of the ruler placed peripherally and abbreviated clues of the mint city.

Fig. 67—Abd Al-Malik Gold Dinar Coin

This coin shows the *Kalima* in the obverse (left image) center field with the mint city, Al Basra, and *darab*, a common word for beat or strike. In the right coin's center is the Qur'anic quotation, "Allah is One, Allah is eternal, He begets not, neither is begotten" (Surah 112). The word *darab* is also found in the Qur'an to introduce a parable, *darab mithal*, or as we say, 'to coin a phrase.' The divine name for "The Eternal," As Samad, on this coin, is found only in Surah 112 and is rarely found in other Arabic religious literature which is discussed in my 1999 publication.[9] The ninety-nine names for that book were extracted from the popular list of names available in a current book authored by al-Ghazali (d. AD 1111) and introduced by Abu Haraira, a contemporary of Muhammad, and an inimitable source of hadiths of the prophet. He was reported to have remarked about the names of God: "God great and glorious has ninety-names, one hundred minus one; single, He loves odd numbers, and whoever enumerates them will enter paradise."[10]

When Dionysius' divine names were examined earlier, a specific feature of naming an attribute with positive connotations, such as The Manifest, was paired with its opposite, The Hidden. Dionysius based this negative, apophatic theology on 1 Kings 19:12 when the prophet Elijah could not hear the Lord God passing by in the clamor of earthquakes and thunderous winds, but he heard the still small voice. The names of God in the Islamic tradition, possibly collected by someone like Waraqa or Abu Haraira, included ten paired names that signify opposite meanings. Two names, "The Manifest" and "The Hidden," appear on a thirteenth-century (642–656 AH) North African gold coin, along with six other names that are on the al-Ghazali list.

Fig. 68—North African Merinid Gold Dinar

9. Bentley, *99 Beautiful Names*, 68.
10. Al-Ghazali, *Ninety-nine Names of God*, 49

Divine names such as "The Restrainer" and "The Expander" are striking examples of the paired opposites that are mentioned throughout the Qur'an. Other names include: "The Giver of Life," "The Giver of Death," "The Expeditor," and "The Delayer." "The First" and "The Last" have close associations with biblical terms. "The Manifest" and "The Hidden" will have a scintillating effect on Islamic mysticism, known as Sufism. Allah's names, "The Delayer" and "The Distresser" are opposites with an affinity toward "Kindness" and "Severity," in Romans 11:22.

"In the name of God, The Gracious and Merciful" are the two beautiful names which serve as a preface to 113 out of 114 Surahs. From early Umayyad reforms to modern times, *bismallah ar-rahmann ar-rahim* appears on coins and currency in the Muslim world as part of the *Kalima*. Surah 59 introduces the first fourteen of the names, while most of the other names appear either singly or more likely coupled with another name. This Surah ends: "To him belong the most beautiful names *(alasama'a alhusna')* to Him praises whatever is in the heavens and on the earth. He is the Mighty One, the Wise."[11] These two names are found in Surah 27:9, 10, recounting the time when Moses throws down his staff that becomes a writhing serpent in Pharaoh's court. Among other more common names for God are: "The Forgiving," "Supreme One," "The Hearer," "The All-Seeing," "The Most High," "The Just," "The Eternal," "The One," and "The Powerful." Many of these appear on coins, including "All-Knowing" (*Al-'Alim*; see Appendix A). The "All Knowing" name hints of Gnosticism which the prophet's cousin, the priest Waraqa, favored as a leader in a monotheistic sect, such as the El Kesaites.

St. Ephrem the Syriac theologian-poet's topics make appearances in the Qur'an. His hymns and homilies are reported by Lebanese scholar, Joseph Aziz, in various editions of his Arabic text, *Priest and Prophet (Qiss wa Nabi)*.[12] The garden of Eden, the last days, and visions of hell were among their mutual interests despite the more than 200 years separating the Qur'an's revelations from Ephrem's joyous compositions. Both alluded to paradise by mentioning the blessed conditions of the inhabitants' clothing and food, even the fine wine of heaven. Ephrem could have sung this hymn for the miracle at the wedding in Cana (John 2:1–11). Ephrem's biographer, Sebastian Brock, toasts this wedding's special guest, Jesus:

---

11. Qur'an 59:22–24, 1449–50.
12. Aziz, *Priest and Prophet*, 132.

I have invited You, Lord, to a wedding feast of song, but the wine—the utterance of praise—at our feast has failed. You the guest, who filled the jars with good wine, fill my mouth with Your Praise.[13]

Youths and maidens will serve fruit, meat, and goblets of nonintoxicating wine,[14] and will sit on towering thrones in the Qur'anic paradise.[15] One Muslim coin declared a warning message: the province of Banijurid in modern Afghanistan issued an oversize, multiple *dirham* in 378 AH, with this threat directed at Christians who buried their gold and silver rather than spending it in the way of Allah.[16]

Fig. 69—Banijurid Large Well Worn Arabic Coin

Jerusalem's most iconic structure is the golden Dome of the Rock, the oldest standing structure of Islam which Muslims identify with the ascent of the prophet Muhammad to the seventh heaven.

---

13. Brock, *Luminous Eye*, 124.
14. Qur'an 56:18, 1410.
15. Qur'an 56:34, 1411.
16. Qur'an 9:34, 447.

Fig. 70—Jerusalem Dome of the Rock

The original intent of this non–mosque shrine, however, was to celebrate the victory of Islam over Christianity, not Judaism, in the sacred space close to the Church of the Holy Sepulchre, whose domes are almost identical in size. Caliph Abd al-Malik ordered the construction of this shrine to replace ruins that once honored martyred Christians and a former church. Christian and Sasanian artisans were brought in from newly captured Persian territories to adorn the walls with mosaic inscriptions (see Fig. 61) alongside the Qur'an's version of Jesus' unfulfilled resurrection:

> O Allah, bless your messenger and Your Servant Jesus, son of Mary. Peace be upon him the day he was born and the day he dies, and the day he shall be raised alive! Such was Jesus, son of Mary.[17]

---

17. Dome of the Rock's version of Qur'an 19:33, 751.

9

Abbasid Rise and Fall
Political Drifts, Spiritual Uplifts

Enter you here, in peace and security, and we shall remove from their hearts any lurking sense of injury. (They will be) like brothers facing each other on thrones, no sense of fatigue shall touch them, nor shall they (ever)be asked to leave.[1]

THIS VERSE FROM THE Qur'an is on a silver *dirham* that quotes Zubaida, the wife of Caliph Harun al-Rashid, who fathered two sons as potential heirs to his throne. Queen Zubaida was concerned for her Arab son in her call for unity in 185 AH, when the following was added to the coin's margin: "Among the things that the mother of the Heir to the Caliphate at the hands of Yasir, blessing come from God."[2]

Fig. 71—Abbasid Dirham of Queen Zubaida

1. Coin's citation from Qur'an 15:46-48, 627.
2. Album, *Checklist of Islamic Coins*, 53.

The Islamic capital moved eastward from Damascus to Baghdad on the Tigris River, after the Abbasids defeated the Umayyads. The new caliphate held on to the Umayyad conquests from Afghanistan to North Africa, but rather than military expansions, the Abbasids made their mark by energizing Islamic spiritual and legal entities. An eastern sect of the Orthodox Church, improbably named Nestorian and receiving no government patronage, endured along with Jews and Christians as peoples of the book. Christian theologians and Jewish rabbis often joined Muslim scholars in discussions and occasionally debated one another in Baghdad. The Islamic legal systems, developed in the second and third centuries after the advent of Islam, prevail today within four schools of traditional Sunnah and one Shi'a school. The five judicial systems applied Aristotelian rationalism to what the Qur'an prescribes as acceptable and forbidden behaviors. The Hadith defined the teachings and actions of Muhammad, but traces of Greek philosophy would be dismissed. This transformation was enhanced by the authoritative voice of al-Ghazali, who wrote his epics against the philosophers during a lifetime of following Islam that began in mystical Sufism. Al-Ghazali concluded with an endorsement of *Kalaam*, or Sunnah orthodoxy. He was born and buried in Tus (see Appendix B), where a small groundmarker identifies his burial in the shadow of a memorial to the Persian national poet Ferdowsi, who died about a hundred years before him. Ferdowsi's *Shahnameh* is faithfully recited by Iranian pilgrims passing through the Mashhad complex shrine of the eighth Shi'a Imam, Ali ar-Rida, less than 20 miles from Tus. Ar-Rida died suddenly in the year 203 AH/ AD 818 in Tus, where he was buried, with a later reburial in Mashhad.

Al-Ghazali's reflections on the ninety-nine names broadened the interpretations of the names when he added personal remarks regarding most of these attributes, beginning with the greatest name, Allah.[3] Transcendence of Allah, the Almighty, is the dominant theology within Islam, but Al-Ghazali tactfully displays God's immanence as apportioned to humankind.

> Man's share in this name should be for him to become god-like [ta'allah], by which I mean that his heart and his aspiration be taken up with Allah—great and glorious.[4] Al-Quddus... The Holy

---

3. The names of God are infinite, but the number 99 is based upon a tradition of Abu Hurayra, companion of Muhammad.

4. Al-Ghazali, *Ninety-nine Names of God*, 52.

is one who transcends every one of the attributes of perfection which the majority of creatures think of perfection.[5]

Al-Qabid (The Restrainer) and *Al-Basit* (The Expander) are combined in one human manifestation echoing apophatic proverbs and parables from previous Scriptures. "He also appropriates alms from the rich and extends sustenance to the weak."[6]

> *Al-Khabir,* (The Aware)... Man's share in this name lies in his being aware of what goes on in his world. His world is his heart, his body and the hidden things by which his heart is characterized by deception and treachery...harboring evil intent while putting on a good front.[7]

Additionally, *Al-Muqaddim* (The Promoter) and *Al-Mu'akhkhir* (The Postponer) are two opposing manifestations that are readily recognizable in mankind. Al-Ghazali simply states, "Man's shares in these attributes of actions is obvious, so we will not occupy ourselves with reiterating it for every name, for fear of prolixity."[8] Al-Ghazali's concept of wisdom left a profound impact on the *Ulema* (The Knowers), the official and unofficial religious and political leaders of all branches of Islam. Less than a hundred years after his death, another master of Islamic thought was born in Balkh, present-day Afghanistan. Jalal al-Din Rumi's global reputation as a Sufi is based upon more than 60,000 verses that are cited in coffee-table-sized books in scores of languages.[9] Rumi followed in the footsteps of his father, a teacher of Islamic law. The family fled their homeland when Rumi was a youth during the early raids of Mongols led by Genghis Khan along the southern branches of the Central Asian Silk Road. As a preacher and teacher, Rumi's fame spread from the Asia Minor city of Konya after he applied his Sufism to theological subjects. Rumi's verses abound with the names of God highlighting the mystery of the divine beloved, referred to in the Qur'an as a Hidden Treasure that needs to be claimed. Rumi's translator, William Chittick, posed a significant question that connects the Infinite Creator with the finite creation which Rumi answered:

---

5. Al-Ghazali, *Ninety-nine Names of God*, 59.
6. Al-Ghazali, *Ninety-nine Names of God*, 81.
7. Al-Ghazali, *Ninety-nine Names of God*, 98, 99.
8. Al-Ghazali, *Ninety-nine Names of God*, 133.
9. Chittick, *Sufi Path of Love*, 5.

"Why did God create the world?" The answer is clear: in order to manifest His own names and Attributes... God says, "I was a Hidden Treasure, so I wanted to be known." In other words, "I created the whole of the universe, and the goal in all of it is to make Myself manifest, sometimes through Gentleness and sometimes through Severity."[10]

The list of the Gentle and Severe names revolves around Rumi's coupling of *Al-Latif*, (The Gentle name) with *Al-Qahhar* (The Overcomer). *Al-Qahir* was the name that the Fatimid Dynasty adopted for its capital in Cairo and where the Shi'a Isma'ili Dynasty built many of the famous landmarks, including the Al-Azhar mosque. The Fatimids introduced a new gold coin design of concentric circles (see Appendix A). They were deposed by Saladin in 909 AH and Cairo today remains a symbol of victory and defeat. For the winners, Qahir is victory, while to the losers, it symbolizes defeat; a single city going in opposite directions. The Abbasid Caliphate in Baghdad was threatened by rival rulers during this time when a caliph who held on for two years (932–934) claimed al-Qahir as his name. A gold coin proclaimed one of the most severe names of God, *Al-Muntaqim* (The Avenger) for his title when Abbasid powers were languishing.

Fig. 72—Caliph Al-Qahir Coin

Rumi's names of God dismissed the negativism of the equal gods of dualism, good and evil. He restated classical Islamic *Kalaam* in poetical forms rather than confront a new faith, Manicheism, which was ready-made to replace the fading remnants of Zoroastrianism. Rumi contended that the Gentle names overcame the Severe names. Mercy overcoming wrath is also

---

10. Chittick, *Sufi Path of Love*, 47–48.

a Christian theme, according to Orthodox theologian, Lossky, who credited St. Thomas Aquinas for reducing it thus: "The two ways of Dionysius to one, making negative theology a corrective to affirmative theology."[11] Rumi directed his Sufi followers to empty their minds and wills, even legal and theological thoughts, and allow the inner meanings of the Qur'an to flourish. By using coins as metaphors, Rumi's key term is *fana'* (annihilation):

> No one will find his way to the Court of Magnificence until he is annihilated. You are your own shadow—become annihilated in the rays of the Sun! How long will you look at your shadow? Look also to the Light... His Attributes have naughted my attributes.[12] ... When gold leaves the face of a counterfeit coin and returns to dwell in its own mine, the disgraced copper remains like smoke— but its lover is more black-faced.[13] ... That balanced and harmonious King of the world sees a balanced lover—my face is as yellow as a gold coin so that I will be placed in His Balance.[14]

In 1883, a Hungarian Jew entered Cairo's Al-Azhar, a world center of Sunnah studies. Ignaz Goldziher became the first non-Muslim to enroll as a researcher and found friendship with Muslims, nourished by his faith, according to his book's introduction by Bernard Lewis.[15] Goldziher emphasized that the mystical sources of Sufism can be traced to Christian monasticism, as well as from Indian Buddhist and Hindu holy men. His summary of the often contentious relationship between Sufis and Islam of the law would be understood by Rumi:

> The first patriarchs of the Sufi conception of religion had indeed assigned a higher value to the "works of the heart" than to the formal observance of Islamic law—"the works of the limbs" as they put it—but they did not declare the latter to be worthless... They did believe that the works of the limbs acquired their value and meaning only in the presence of, and in concert with, the works of the heart.[16]

---

11. Lossky, *Mystical Theology of the Eastern Church*, 26.
12. Chittick, *Sufi Path of Love*, 179.
13. Chittick, *Sufi Path of Love*, 203.
14. Chittick, *Sufi Path of Love*, 209.
15. Goldziher, *Introduction to Islamic Theology*, ix.
16. Goldziher, *Introduction to Islamic Theology*, 147.

Rumi's "works of the heart" meant rejection of hypocrisy, and extended to the breaking of the rosary beads and pawning of prayer rugs.[17] Nevertheless, rosewood beads, despite their origin in Indian Hindu or Buddhist worship, continue to be reflexively turned in the right hand of Muslims who privately or publicly recite the ninety-nine beautiful names of God.

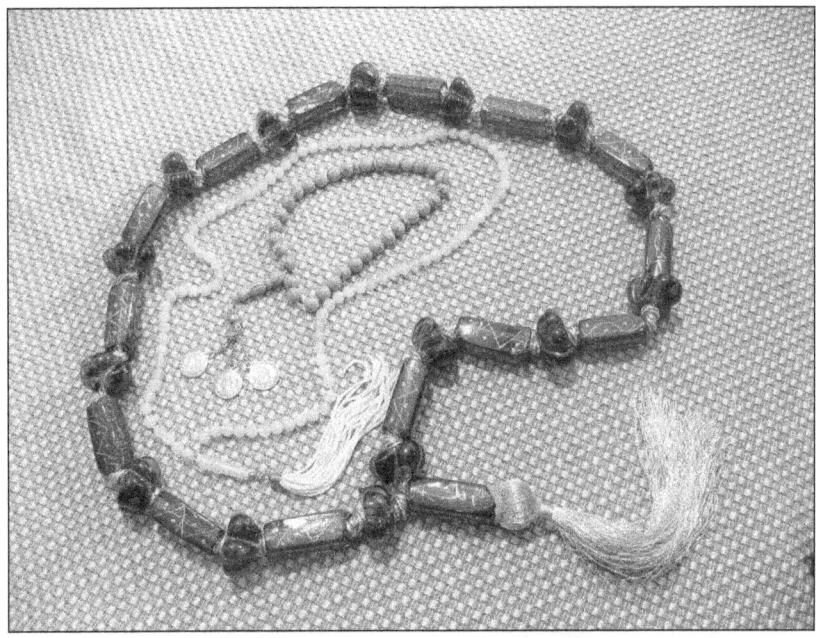

Fig. 73—Muslim Rosary of 99 Beads

Following Rumi, Ibn Taymiyah and his family fled the advancing Mongols who attacked their home town of Harran when he was six years old. Complementing al-Ghazali, he was a fiercely independent thinker, but exalted the orthodox standards of Muhammad's prophethood and nationhood. The Kingdom of Saudi Arabia as a Wahhabi theocratic nation is linked to this twelfth-century lawyer who survived multiple prison terms until his death in Damascus. In Cairo, where he was also a political prisoner of the ruling Turkish sultans, the Mamluks, he faced the Crusader and Mongol invaders. These groups were not the object of Ibn Taymiyah's insistence on the return to the days under the prophet Muhammad and his successors, the original "rightly guided," *Rashidun*: Abu Bakr, Umar, 'Uthman, and Ali (11–40 AH). His enemies were fellow jurists who objected to Ibn

17. Chittick, *Sufi Path of Love*, 267.

Taymiyah's legal opinions (*fatwas*) based on Muhammad's prophetic ministry.[18] The idea of a nation-state was not addressed in Mecca, but this was not the case in Medina, where the prophet governed as a local leader with universal overtones. His role as the model for his followers was unattainable because of his Qur'anic revelations. His stamp of greatness, "an exalted standard of character," (Qur'an 68:4) was not transferred to Muhammad's successors who faced ongoing, often violent struggles over the question of who was the most worthy to rule as the vicegerent or caliph comparable to King David's reign (see Fig. 63). Contemporary author Tamim Ansary writes regarding the modern manifestation of Salafism:

> Ibn Taymiyah mythologized the perfection of life in that first community, referring to Mohammed's companions as *al-salaf al-salihin*, "the pious (or pristine) originals." ... Versions of his doctrines eventually reemerged in India and North Africa.[19]

Ibn Taymiyah accepted the Mamluk authority. He attacked the Shi'a far more than his fellow Sunnis and was thoroughly anti-Sufi:

> Indeed, ecstatic Sufism (as opposed to "sober Sufism") disturbed Ibn Taymiyah almost as much as pagan invaders, because to him infidels were merely the enemy outside, assaulting Islam, whereas Sufism was the enemy within.[20]

Shrines containing the mutilated bodies of Muhammad's son-in-law Ali, and two grandsons, Hassan and Hussain, are integral to understanding the religious and political separation between Shi'a and Sunnah Muslims. These shrine-tombs, located in southern Iraq, are obligatory for Shi'a pilgrims commemorating Muhammad's family martyrdom in AD 680. Tombs have further divided the Sunnah community when the Wahhabi Saudi dynasty declared burial grounds were idolatrous. The Wahhabi attacks on the Iraqi Shi'a shrines expanded to other regions where graves have been desecrated by Wahhabi sympathizers.[21] The Karbala, Iraq shrine dedicated to Muhammad's grandson, Imam Hussain, is the burial ground for hundreds of Shi'ites every year (see Appendix B).

---

18. Ansary, *Destiny Disrupted*, 161–62.
19. Ansary, *Destiny Disrupted*, 163.
20. Ansary, *Destiny Disrupted*, 165.
21. Momen, *Introduction to Shi'i Islam*, 143.

The heir of Caliph Harun al-Rashid turned out to be Ma'mun (AD 813–833), who opposed the idea that the Qur'an was an uncreated, eternal document, after Aristotle, the Greek philosopher, appeared to him in a dream. According to Garth Fowden, Ma'mun was advised to use his own rational judgment, a precept of Aristotle that the Christian Nestorians had introduced by translating Greek classics first into Syriac, then from Syriac into Arabic.[22] Fowden appeals to Western scholars to rethink their academic biases against the continuity of Greek rationalism in Syriac Christianity that impacted Abbasid philosophical thought. Louth recognizes John the Damascene, who mixed his Greek philosophical and theological positions under the Umayyads to advance Christianity for future centuries[23] (see Fig. 51). A coin minted under al-Ma'mum repeats Surah 30 and is titled *Al Rum* (The Romans). The date of this Surah is the Christian year, 615–616, when the Sasanians under Khusro II attacked Jerusalem (see Fig. 59). This was a humiliating defeat for the Christian forces (*Rum*, New Rome, Constantinople), but a few years later the Byzantine army of Heraclius won back the territories that the Persians had conquered (see Fig. 78). Surah 30 expresses the confidence that the Arabs felt when the two empires, Greek and Persian, were militarily exhausted by centuries of intermittent warfare. This defeat of the Byzantine Empire spoke prophetically for Islam's eventual religious and political victories.

Fig. 74—Abbasid Silver Coin Al Ma'mun

Two prominent names of God are imprinted on this coin:

---

22. Fowden, *Before and after Muhammad*, 157.
23. Louth, *St. John Damascene*, 223.

The Roman Empire has been defeated, in a land close by: But they, (even) after (this) defeat of theirs, will soon be victorious. Within a few years, with Allah is the Decision. In the Past and in the Future on that Day shall the Believers rejoice. With the help of Allah, He helps whom He will and He is exalted in Might (Al-Aziz), Most Merciful (Ar-Rahim).[24]

---

24. Qur'an, 30:2–5, 1008.

10

Manichaeism
Dualism along the Silk Road

ST. AUGUSTINE (AD 354–430) is the most famous religious and political figure to denounce the founder of Manichaeism, known for its amalgamation of Jewish, Christian, Zoroastrian, and Buddhist faiths. Prior to his conversion, Augustine was a devoted follower of this religion that for several centuries had confronted the other faiths. Augustine charged his former religion with dualism, a belief in divine being with two equal natures, light opposed by darkness. In his final years, the sainted Christian asked forgiveness for his burning hatred of his former co-religionists.[1] Manichaeism combined Jesus the Messiah, with the Great King (Matthew 25) and assumed several Buddhist monastic practices. Founder Mani was born in AD 216 into a humble family in Ctesiphon and in his youth was involved in a Jewish-Christian baptistic sect, probably founded by an Arab named El Kasai. Mani left this El Kasaite church after he announced that he was an apostle of light. He traveled widely and wrote books that served a strong missionary force long after his death by crucifixion in AD 276. His enemies included the magian priests who exercised a powerful influence over the Sasanian emperors and the Zoroastrian faithful. Shapur I strengthened his power by arresting Mani after the Sasanians defeated the Roman emperor Decius in AD 250 (see Fig. 47).

The sect endured over 1,000 years in centers far from its original Persian roots. In Southern France during the eleventh century the Albigensians were wiped out by crusades called for by popes and mendicant preachers. Another Manichaean minority, the Bogomiles, survived in Slavic areas until the 1500s. Mani's missionaries followed the Silk Road

---

1. Schaff, *History of the Christian Church*, 3:1012.

where monasteries and local governments were organized by his disciplined priests. The Nestorian Christians, also originating in Persia, thrived in these Central Asian regions and competed with both Manichaeans and Buddhists for adherents among the Turkish, Uighar, and other tribal groups on the Mongolian steppes.

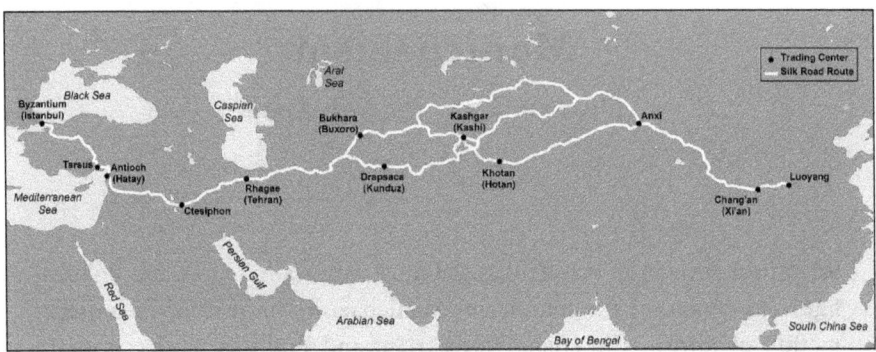

Fig. 75—Map of Silk Road

Recently discovered parchments on the Silk Road compiled in Klimkeit's book include this Parthian hymn portraying Jesus facing Satan:

> Because [of Satan] the elect were chosen by Jesus. Satan wanted to break through the fiery waves, to burn the whole world with fire. The noble ruler (Jesus) changed his garment and appeared before Satan in his power.[2] . . . Awake, brethren, you chosen ones, on this day of the salvation of souls . . . on which Jesus, the Son of God, entered Parinirvana![3]

Parinirvana is a Buddhist term for Jesus' crucifixion and his entry into highest Nirvana. Former messengers Jesus, Zarathustra, and Buddha evoke the Gospels' parable of the sower as it is retold by Mani in a Parthian sermon:

> These two natures are mingled with each other in the course of rebirths, like [wheat] and chaff [that] the farmers separate . . . from one another . . . [The Sower] is also similar to that wheat, and my children are similar to the farmers. . . My mind [and my true] Word are similar to the wind, and the just Law is similar to flail.[4]

2. Klimkeit, *Gnosis on the Silk Road*, 71 (brackets Klimkeit).
3. Klimkeit, *Gnosis on the Silk Road*, 69, 71.
4. Klimkeit, *Gnosis on the Silk Road*, 185.

Persian and Turkish texts for an unknown Uighur king written after AD 850 were scattered in oasis towns in the Taklimakan Desert at a time when a Turkish king ruled over these nomadic people. A prayer offered as part of a New Year's royal ceremony called on this unnamed "King of East," "our divine Khan" and created by the "Word of God":

> May you, (oh King) live. . . in peace and good fortune. May you live forever, you who are created by the Word of God. . .[5]

When the Kushans were forced out of China into Central Asia, they adopted the Indo-Greek mintage style that appeared on coins as *Soter Megas* (Great Savior).[6] An early king, Vima Takha, reigned in what is now Afghanistan from AD 55–105, and his image is on a bronze coin along with a horse and rider.

Fig. 76—Vima Takha Coin

Among Manichacan images of Parthian parables is the uplifted stake with two coiled serpents encapsulating the gnostic theology of evil and good residing in humankind: the Old Man vs the New Man. The New Testament image is of one benevolent serpent coiled around a pole (see Fig. 24). The gnostic Abraxas god with serpent's legs survives today in the medical symbol, the caduceus, which embodies the two serpents. An alternative to Abraxas is the Greek god Mercury and his winged feet and staff.

> [T]wo snakes, one is the person who loves the body, for whom bearing is troublesome, (but) who is unconcerned (about the soul) . . . The second snake is the person for whom the soul is dearer

---

5. Klimkeit, *Gnosis on the Silk Road*, 158.
6. Sayles, *Ancient Coin Collecting*, 92.

than the body. There is very little poison in him and his attachment to the world is weak.[7]

Rituals of multi-baptisms linked the Essenes of the Qumran Dead Sea community with Manichaean daily baths washing away pollutions of the flesh. Both communities subjected their monastic members to vegetarian diets and sexual abstentions. Honoring the poor meant that newcomers would surrender their earthly goods. Strict rules governed the lower auditor ranks who worked in agriculture, which was forbidden for the priestly class.

Another baptistic sect still exists today in the swamps at the mouth of Iraq's rivers. This non-Muslim group is not to be confused with the Sabaeans, who are identified as the early habitants of South Arabia and recalled in the biblical story of the Queen of Sheba visiting Solomon (1 Kgs 10). They are also cryptically folded into The Qur'an and cited with Jews, Christians, and the *Majus*, the common misidentification for all followers of Zoroaster:

> And those who follow the Jewish (scriptures), and the Sabians, Christians, Magicians, and Polytheists, Allah will judge between them on the Day of Judgment: for Allah is witness of all things.[8]

A gold coin of Byzantine King Heraclius and son, along with several Sasanian coins, comprise a small part of the Aurel Stein collection in Helen Wang's research of Oriental coinage. Wang lists a Sasanian *drachm* that covered the eyes of a female body and several imitation gold Byzantine coins from bodies in tombs[9] which once had been displayed in jewelry.

---

7. Klimkeit, *Gnosis on the Silk Road*, 182–83.
8. Qur'an 22:17, 825.
9. Wang, *Money on the Silk Road*, 239.

MANICHAEISM

Fig. 77—Sasanian Khusro I Drachm

Fig. 78—Heraclius Gold Coin, Jewelry

Grave robbers notwithstanding, Helen Wang searches the money trail left by tradesmen which involved the Polo brothers in the thirteenth century and explorer Aurel Stein in the early years of the twentieth century. Marco Polo recorded his Chinese Silk Road journey, which ended in 1292 after a seventeen-year employment in the court of Kublai Khan. The Great Khan of the Mongols employed foreigners as tax assessors, and Marco was tasked with this work in the southern, non-Mongolian Chinese markets where silk and salt were paid for with paper or bronze coins called "cash." The Tang dynasty coin was issued by a rebel before his own troops killed him.

Fig. 79—Chinese Coin, Cash, Tang Dynasty

Polo's biographer, Laurence Bergreen, describes Marco's journey down the Grand Canal connecting modern-day Beijing with Hangzhou where he was the overseer of the lucrative salt markets. Bergreen imagines young Polo reflecting on the bridge that now bears his name:

> ... The Grand Canal became a unified entity for the ... Emperor Yang Ti in AD 604. Over the next six years, three million laborers expanded the Grand Canal, largely by hand. The sacrifice was enormous; half the workforce perished ... the dynasty collapsed as a result. But the canal survived.[10]

The Nestorians were belatedly honored in this imperial kingdom, located in the heart of Han China. This was after centuries of missionary and commercial expeditions, beginning in the northern steppe lands among the Mongolian and Uighar tribes. After the demise of the Mongols, the Nestorians and the Manichaean populations—both Persian, and thus foreign faiths—were replaced by Buddhism and later Islam. The Nestorians erected a monument in AD 780 that hailed the honorable Jesus the Messiah, in Chinese and Syriac characters and with images that the Buddhists understood. A cross is prominently centered on this sketch of the Xi'an Nestorian stele.

---

10. Bergreen, *Marco Polo*, 209.

MANICHAEISM

Fig. 80—Nestorian Monument Tang Dynasty

Contemporary scholar Li Tang assesses the Christian presence in China following the Mongol destruction of Baghdad in 1258:

> Christianity flourished along the Silk Roads from the Oxus to the Chinese shores. The 13th and early 14th centuries were the heyday of the Church of the East. It was geographically the largest Christian Church of the Middle Ages with its center in Baghdad.[11]

The archaeological evidence for the Christians consists mostly of tombstone markers that are currently being studied. Mani's Asian disciples disappeared with scant traces, typically in the form of critiques left by their enemies. The Nestorian Christians' historic communities are memorialized by missionary historian, Philip Jenkins, who writes about the growth of Christianity in areas where the church was declared extinct. He interprets the millions of new Chinese believers as a significant sign of recovery:

> Perhaps the Nestorians were tempted to write off their Chinese missions as having failed forever, but as we have seen, forever can be a risky term to apply to human affairs, and so can extinction. And even if particular denominations or churches perish, Christian believers do in fact return, and flourish.[12]

---

11. Tang, *From the Oxus River*, 5.
12. Jenkins, *Lost History of Christianity*, 255–56.

11

Turks, Crusaders, Mongols
Outlanders Besiege Arab Muslims

BEGINNING IN THE EIGHTH century, waves of Turkish migrants from Central Asian steppes followed their chiefs and unfurled their tribal colors only to exchange them for Muslim flags in what is now modern Turkey. In the twenty-first century, Turks act as borders or bridges distinguishing Islam from the West. The final of three caliphates, the Ottoman, was abolished at the end of World War I by Kamel Ataturk. He set in motion an elected republican form of government which dramatically eliminated palaces and the authority of the sultan-caliph. The sultanate was a Turkish fiefdom centuries before the Ottoman Turks inherited the caliphate from the Abbasids after 1453. The Seljuks are a model of how the migratory Turkish clans coalesced to absorb Anatolia and other Byzantine provinces after the Orthodox and Latin churches split the Roman Empire. Byzantine mints left behind an engraved image of the famed Christ the Pantocrator holding the gospel, which appeared on coins issued by Fakhr al-Din Arslan (AD 1144–1174).

Fig. 81—Christ Pantocrator Byzantine Symbol

Other pictographic figures originating in former Byzantine Asia Minor were on coins minted by the Artuqids and Zengids and are featured in two separate volumes authored by Spengler and Sayles.¹ The Seljuk Turks dominated during the tumultuous twelfth and thirteenth centuries when a rare Seljuq of Rum coin was minted naming the Abbasid Caliph. The coin's obverse features a turbaned horseman spearing a panther. A coin featuring St. George slaying a dragon was minted in 1822 when King George IV was on the British throne.

Fig. 82—Spearing Seljuk, St. George

Coins with the double-headed eagle appeared on a *dirham* minted in the city of Amid by the Artuqid Turks when they became vassals to Saladin.² The Polish double eagle is ready to take flight to the Russian Empire to become her national symbol under Czar Nicolas I (1825–1855).

Fig. 83—Double Eagle, Seljuk, Poland

1. Spengler, *Turkoman Figural Bronze Coins*, 2:6.
2. Spengler, *Turkoman Figural Bronze Coins*, 1:2.

Lions pause under the Sun's rays stamped on a Seljuk gold dinar (Fig. 84) and a silver *dirham* (shown in Appendix A). This Seljuk of Rum coin was minted in Konya in AD 1241 and the Persian dinar's date is 1896, minted in St. Petersburg for Muzaffar al Din Shah.

Fig. 84—Seljuk, Iranian Lion Coins

Numismatic authors Spengler and Sayles provide details on these coins in the first volume, suggesting some reasons that human figures were stamped on coins when traditional Muslims forbade that practice. Their second volume covers Turkish rule in the same area of southeastern Turkey and Iraq where a sizeable Nestorian Christian minority community lived. The coins' pictorial features are associated with a specific geographical region's history and its religious dissenters, beginning with Abraham, who passed through Haran on the way to Palestine (see Fig. 11). Roadways used by Alexander's soldiers and Greek philosophers connected Haran with Persia and Central Asia and centuries later these roads linked Baghdad to Edessa and the Christian seminary town of Nisibin, and described by Spengler as follows:

> Nisibin was not only a center for theological training, but one of culture as well. The Nestorian community there regularly served as a provider of physicians, teachers, scribes, and accountants for the Caliphate . . . In addition to their cultural advancements, the Nestorians of Nisibin were a relatively wealthy group. During the Caliphate of Mansur, the city's Bishop built a new church at a cost of 56,000 gold dinars.[3]

---

3. Spengler, *Turkoman Figural Bronze Coins*, 2:xxi.

Encroaching on this Christian intellectual, cultural, and commercial region were Crusaders from the West and Genghis Khan's Mongolian invasion from the East. The wearied Turks spent years fighting Arabs, including the greatest of all warriors, the Kurd Saladin. He recaptured Jerusalem and offered chivalrous terms to his European enemies, vastly different than the massacres that the Crusaders had committed against Arab Jerusalem ninety years earlier. The mounted knights and foot soldiers of Europe advanced as far as Edessa by 1098, but after Crusader in-fighting and withdrawal of Armenian support, Edessa returned to Muslim control a half-century later. Saladin's prolonged attacks and his retaking Jerusalem followed the Crusaders' fatal loss at the battle of Hattin, July 4, 1187, a very hot day for the knights under their heavy armor. With Jerusalem back in Muslim hands, Saladin re-installed the Greeks in the holy places and expelled the Crusaders who would regroup in a small number of seacoast towns, including Acre and Tyre.

Fig. 85—Saladin Dirham Damascus Mint

Crusader occupation did not involve a perpetual holy war and plundering, but days and years of amicable contacts between East and West, Muslims, Jews, and Christians. Contemporary author Zachary Karabell recalls the factors of coexistence that do not get into history books, romance novels, and movies. As Karabell reports, religion was the battle-hardened fixture during these centuries while intermarriages, immigration, markets, and international trade all were fostering ordinary personal contacts between the days of battles for Aleppo, Jerusalem, Acre, and the hundreds of other towns on the eastern Mediterranean shores.[4]

---

4. Karabell, *Peace be upon You*, 105–7.

Meanwhile back in the Gobi Desert in AD 1162, the Year of the Swine in the Zodiac calendar of the Twelve Beasts, a son was born into a Mongolian family. He would eventually rule half of the known world under the name of Genghis Khan. His leadership style was ruthless, often marked by violent rages, yet he retained his troops by successful conquests rewarded by rich booty. Peace was extended toward his own civilian populations and his captive people. This debased silver *dirham* is an example of a Genghis Khan coin, minted at the Damascus mint and citing the Abbasid Caliph, Nasr al-Din.

Fig. 86—Genghis Khan Coin Cites Caliph

Harold Lamb presents the Khan's Great Seal's (*Yassa*) covenant:

> The first law of the *Yassa* is rather remarkable. "It is ordered that all men should believe in one God, creator of Heaven and earth, the sole giver of goods and poverty, of life and death as pleases Him, whose power over all things is absolute."[5]

Lamb pointed out that the backstory of the Great Seal began with Christians of the Nestorian Church of the East dispersed among the Mongolians. They were members of the military, as were the Khan's sons who had Nestorian wives. On the fateful two-year campaign through Central Asia to the Caspian, the Muslim Turks were the object of Khan's wrath, ignited when the Turkish and thoroughly Sunna shah massacred the Mongols' trade delegation. An unidentified Persian filed this disturbing dispatch.

> "Have you never heard that a band of men from the place where the sun rises, overrode the earth to the Caspian Gates, carrying destruction among peoples and sowing death in its passage? Then,

---

5. Lamb, *Genghis Khan*, 59.

returning to its master—it arrived sound and hale, loaded with booty. And this in less than two years."[6]

The Mongol Dynasty came back for several assaults on Muslims that reached its murderous climax in the destruction of Baghdad under Hulagu, a grandson of Genghis, in 1258. Hulagu annexed Mosul, north of Baghdad, where an independent Zengid Dynasty ruled. The Zengids were descendants of Badr al din Lu'Lu'id, a former Armenian slave (see Appendix A). Hulagu's brother, Kublai Khan, who inherited his grandfather's empire, reached out to non-Mongolians to govern his far-reaching kingdom. Marco Polo, an Italian merchant's son, served as a tax consultant in China during this time. The last of the Mongols, renamed Mughals, converted to Islam and built a major Indian empire that endured until the British Raj displaced them in the late eighteenth century. The spiritual posterity of these Mongolian invaders includes nearly two-thirds of the world's contemporary Muslim population: Indian, Pakistani, Bangladeshi, and Indonesian. Sufi teachers, often elevated to the level of saints, were quietly and peacefully introducing Islam to these southwest Asian peoples.

Francis of Assisi and Muhyiddin Ibn 'Arabi both achieved saintly status in the thirteenth century AD. These two European pilgrims landed on Arab shores during the close of the Fifth Crusade. In 1219, the year that Genghis Khan opened his two-year blitz through Afghanistan and Persia, Francis joined the Crusaders in Damietta, a Nile port, where he seized the opportunity to explain his Christian faith to the Sultan of Egypt. Francis kept his vow of poverty by allegedly rejecting the Sultan's gifts. When the defeated Crusaders sailed back to Europe they had no pieces of the True Cross as Greek priests hid the pieces in Jerusalem. Francis' delayed departure allowed him to visit Palestinian cities where his Franciscan brothers remain to the present day. Once back in Italy, Francis wrote letters to his fellow priests and European leaders in which he expressed his admiration for the Saracens' daily prayers, their devotion to God's name, and the personal contacts that he had made in the enemy's camp. Among the scores of modern St. Francis biographers is J. Hoeberichts, who attributes the future saint's expanding vision of God to his contacts with Muslims in Damietta:

> On the basis of his personal experience, Francis placed over against this negative attitude his much more positive theological vision of Islam. All the good that he had discovered in Islam, had its origin in God, the source of all good. It was because of the presence of

6. Lamb, *Genghis Khan*, 135.

all these good features which came from God and which he gratefully wanted to return to God. . . . In his reverence for the Koran, Francis stood practically alone in his time.[7]

Ibn 'Arabi, the Andalusian Haji, was enjoying his safety in the upper Euphrates River Valley city of Malata in 619 AH. Clusters of Christians survived in this region that offered protection and where Ibn 'Arabi might have met a refugee family fleeing the Mongol invaders. The family's young son will be universally known as Rumi, who along with Ibn 'Arabi, was destined to be one of the two greatest avatars of Sufism. Ibn 'Arabi's Sufism began with mystics who introduced their fellow Muslim to the spiritual disciplines of a Spanish order. Spain at this time was undergoing major shifts as the Muslims were slowly driven southward by the Christian kingdom's *Reconquista* replacing the Moorish emirs.

Fig. 87—Andalusian Coin Moors Decline

Ibn 'Arabi's departure from the Iberian Peninsula led to a career of itineration with his manuscripts and pilgrimages in North Africa, Mecca, Jerusalem, Aleppo, and Damascus, where he died and is buried (see Appendix B).

The troubles following the Crusader years left the Europeans blocked from pilgrimage sites, but with acquired tastes for sugar, spices, and fine cloths that had passed through multiple Mediterranean ports. Columbus' alternate route to the New World took place in 1492, the year of the expulsion of the last Muslim emir, along with the forced exodus of non-Christians, Jews, and Muslims from Spain. A softer side of the *Reconquista* was portrayed in the spirituality of St. Therese of Avila and her protégé,

---

7. Hoeberichts, *Francis and Islam*, 93.

John of the Cross (d. 1605). Despite the 300 years separating John from Ibn 'Arabi, there are parallel subjects like the names of God and John's spirituality of the heart that harmonized with Ibn 'Arabi's absorption of these subjects. Ibn 'Arabi's most recognizable verses were first composed while in Mecca after 598 AH:

> My heart has become capable of every form: it is a pasture for gazelles and a convent for Christian monks./And a temple for idols and the pilgrim's Ka'ba and the tables of the Torah and the book of the Qur'an./I follow the religion of Love: whatever way Love's camels take, that is my religion and my faith.[8]

The Meccan verses and his other writings have not always been accepted in the Muslim world, as riots in Cairo as late as 1999 have borne out. Condemnatory charges of pantheism led to an Egyptian government ban against his books in 1979. Biographer Stephen Hirtenstein registered this defense of Ibn 'Arabi:

> In the name of Truth, the authorities restricted access to one whose life was dedicated to the universality of divine Compassion. It is sad to note that hardly any of the people who argued so vehemently against Ibn 'Arabi had ever read his works in detail.[9]

For St. John of the Cross, the human heart is an organ for understanding Sufism and Christian spirituality because it is an organ of change, as Luce Lopez-Baralt summarizes:

> Both St. John and Ibn 'Arabi have a heart—a *qalb* or "*galibo*"—colorless and as pure as water . . . with a protean ability to reflect in its perpetually moving "silvery features" the continuous manifestations which the Deity makes of Its own essence to itself in the blessed soul that is able to assume any form. Somehow St. John of the Cross must have been familiar with this "knowledge of the secret of the movements of the heart."[10]

Lopez-Baralt shares another view of the heart's inverted or mirror images: the Known and Unknowable God. The divine names, which reflect the yin and yang of God's attributes, kindness and severity, return to apophatic themes of this book:

---

8. Lopez-Baralt, "St. John of the Cross," 76.
9. Hirtenstein, *Unlimited Mercifier*, 242–43.
10. Lopez-Baralt, "St. John of the Cross," 78.

Power and majesty are clearly the "yang" side of divine reality, while beauty and wisdom are the "yin" side. If the first are observed in God, it is because He is incomparable and distant. On the contrary, the created world manifests beauty and wisdom because it is a reflection of God, and shows His proximity and similarity [to God].[11]

The travels of Marco Polo intersect with Genghis Khan and the Crusaders in Acre during their final Frankish kingdom where the seventeen-year-old Marco waited with his father and uncle before their long trek across the Asian continent. The family traveled with pilgrims on a ship from their Venice home and later joined throngs of Christians in Jerusalem in 1270 where the Polos insisted that they were businessmen, according to Bergreen.[12] The two senior Polos had accomplished a similar trip to China and secured documents from Genghis Khan for a return journey. The great Khan had requested holy oil from the Church of the Holy Sepulchree and 100 Christians to teach his people. They secured the holy oil, but only two friars were enlisted to join the Polos, and even these failed to complete the trip to the court of Genghis Khan. Since the time when Acre was first conquered by Richard the Lion-Hearted during the First Crusade in 1191, this port city had established strong commercial relationships with Europe and its mint turned out specious gold coins for both local and international trade. Richard spent enormous amounts for his own ransom during the First Crusade. In October 1187, he paid 50,000 bezants to rescue relics that were stored in the Church of the Holy Sepulchre when Saladin reconquered Jerusalem.[13] Crusaders minted a series of gold bezants that crudely imitated the Egyptian *dinar* and the Muslim *Kalima* (see Appendix A).

---

11. Murata, *Tao of Islam*, 247.
12. Bergreen, *Marco Polo*, 41.
13. Schaff, *History of the Christian Church*, 5:251.

Fig. 88—Crusader Coin Imitates Arab

Arabic numerals, once rejected by popes and Christian kings, were adopted by Western commercial and academic interests following the recommendation of mathematician Leonardo Fibonacci of Pisa.

In AD 1291, Acre surrendered to the sultan of Egypt who ordered the killing of most of the port's residents. However, Acre's demise continued for the local Palestinian merchants who depended on European markets and Holyland travelers. By the end of the fifteenth century, the pilgrimages to Jerusalem were slowed to a near halt. This convinced Columbus and the court of Ferdinand and Isabella to open the sea route for commercial and missionary ventures to sail west to arrive at the exotic east.

12

Antiquity in US Coins

"In God We Trust"

Precious metals were hammered into pictographic objects called coins as early as 700 BC in the Greek Asia Minor province of Lydia. The earliest mints used primitive craftsmanship located near places where gold could be gathered from the surface after rains had eroded it from its primary deposits and sent it down along streams and rivers. A Pompeii wall painting uncovered from the Mt. Vesuvius eruption (AD 79) reveals a Roman mint with seven winged cupids playfully striking, weighing, inspecting, and firing an oven inside a villa (see Fig. 33). The ancient mints were far different from the modern mints with heavy equipment stamping out manufactured coins by the millions; using metals extracted out of deep mines, continents away from the Philadelphia, Denver, and San Francisco mints.

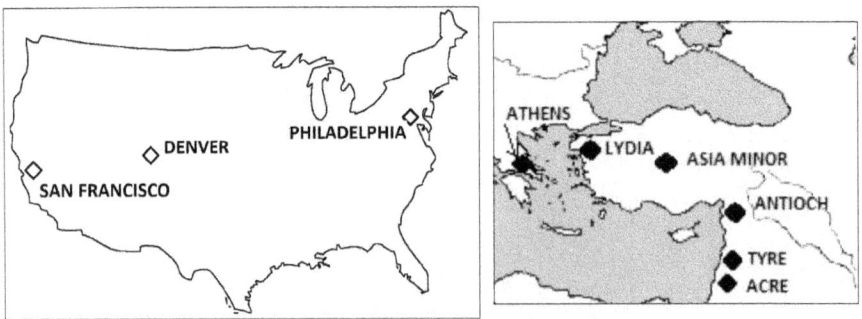

Fig. 89—Ancient Eurasian, Modern United States Mints

However, today the striking, weighing, firing, and inspecting of manufactured coins still follow the basic handmade process of antiquity. New metals, along with bronze, silver, and gold, are incorporated as alloys to strengthen the two-sided, head-and-tail, yin-and-yang space. Coinmaking in household mints in the ancient world continues to have a certain ring that echoes throughout all modern mints, including the change in our pockets.

On a coin's obverse side, whether it's Alexander, Tiberius Caesar, Lincoln, or Kennedy in their life's prime, their faces assume eternal deified omniscience. On that same side dates become apparent, suggesting the ending of a life or dynasty. All living things have expiration dates and coins are conspicuous avatars of "from womb to tomb." Once the United States won its independence from Great Britain and established a nonmonarchial republic, she was free from any European official laws of royal heraldry that determined who and what would be engraved on a coin, as well as where something would be engraved on the coin. The US minters looked back at the classical Greek and Roman coins for models and a few were awarded prime-time exposure, which included the Roman Republic sun god, Sol, and Athena, patron goddess of Athens. Athenian Owl *tetradrachms* remained in international circulation from 500 BC to AD 1500. On this coin, olive leaves appear with a single berry to the right of the owl. The olive branches are surprisingly visible on dollar bills, perhaps due to the fact that the US olive tree is a wild olive and a nonnative tree. Globally it is a symbol of peace. The olive leaves with berries are stamped on the United States dollar and are found on the border of the bill's face side. On the reverse side, look at the Great Seal and the eagle facing toward the quiver where the olive branch is located.

Fig. 90—Greek Coin, US Dollar Olive Leaves

When the apostle Paul wrote a letter to Christians in Rome, he asked his gentile readers to imagine that they were comparable to a wild olive branch whose root source was biblical Israel. Paul then issued a severe reminder to these non-Jewish converts in Rome:

> But if some of the branches were broken off, and you, a wild olive shoot, were grafted in their place to share the richness of the olive tree, do not boast over the branches. If you do boast, remember it is not you that support the root, but the root that supports you.[1]

The Athenian Owl *tetradrachm* with the sacred wild olive sprig was not the only coin that was in Paul's money bag while he was writing the Romans letter shortly after AD 50 during an extended stay in the Greek port city of Corinth. He had longer periods in the Syrian city of Antioch between his gentile mission trips where the bronze coin of Antioch's city goddess, Tyche, was minted and widely circulated throughout these formerly Greek but now-Roman cities. The bust of Tyche, protector of the city of Antioch with her turreted crown, makes its way into modern coinage in the form of Lady Liberty.

Fig. 91—Goddess Tyche, Lady Liberty Dime

In another Pauline letter, Galatians, that was written during Nero's reign (AD 54–68), he refers to liberty when he calls for the Galatians to remain steadfast in their freedom in Christ (Gal 5:1). Lady Liberty was struck in 1904 at the San Francisco mint. The Galatians text refers to free and slave women:

> Now this is an allegory: these women are two covenants. One is from Mount Sinai, bearing children for slavery; she is Hagar. Now Hagar is Mount Sinai in Arabia; she corresponds to the present

1. Rom 11:17–18 RSV.

Jerusalem, for she is in slavery with her children. But the Jerusalem above is free, and she is our mother . . . [2]

"Shekel" was at first a common name for various objects serving as counterweights on scales, and later during biblical times the silver shekel was the Tyre shekel and dedicated to the god Melqarth. Biblical scholar John Bright identifies the Tyrian Ba'al whose priests confronted Elijah at Mt. Carmel.[3] The Melqarth shekels were the infamous thirty pieces of silver paid to Judas when he betrayed Jesus (Matt 26:14–16). Paradoxically, Judas' attempt to return the Syrian silver is blocked by the temple authorities. He tosses the coins on the Temple floor and goes out to hang himself (Matt 27:3–10). The first offering collected by the Christian community, by way of further paradox, is used to buy a pauper's cemetery with these thirty pieces of silver (Acts 1:15–19).

The walking eagle engraved on the silver shekel resembles the eagle on this US half-dollar struck at the San Francisco mint in 1944.

Fig. 92—Eagles on Melqarth and US Coins

The face of the god Melqarth on this Tyrian coin did not restrict its use as the coin of choice to pay the annual Temple tax (see Fig 15). The coin's silver purity and weight added to its commercial and religious values. The Essene community hid these coins in clay jars in caves above the Dead Sea for some future use (see Fig 19). The United States half-dollar eagle, with its wings positioned to take flight, has been a consistent image on the US coin's reverse side. During the Roman Republic days (44–28 BC), the sun god Sol's bust was stamped on a coin's obverse. The rays emanating from

2. Gal 4:24–26 RSV.
3. Bright, *History of Israel*, 227n.

the head are reminders of the deified Egyptian Akhenaton (see Fig. 04) and the gnostic gods, Abraxas and Ialdabaoth (see Figs 42 and 46). The sun god's radiant beams are no match for the United States Peace Dollar, whose radiant crown on the obverse side and the standing eagle on the reverse are awash with the sun's rays. By way of contrast, the Statue of Miss Liberty guards the New York harbor under a crown of seven rays.

Fig. 93—Roman Republic Sun God, US Peace Dollar

This silver Peace Dollar was minted in San Francisco in 1934.

A coin struck in AD 97 in the reign of Roman Emperor Nerva honored Pontius Pilate, the former governor of Judea, who presided over the trial of Jesus leading to his crucifixion. The four Gospels present a record of Pilate's behavior during this fateful day (Mark 15:1–15). This coin was from an obscure Asia Minor Provincial mint, and like the Antiochian Tyche, it was bronze, as silver and gold were restricted to Roman mints. Three barley sheaves and stems of wheat are recognized symbols that are struck on many world coins. Jesus' parable of the sower from the Gospel of Matthew (chapter 13) is an example of universal aspirations, multiple harvests, and bread.

Fig. 94—Pontius Pilate Bronze Prutah, US Copper Cent

The wheat on the reverse of the one cent was first issued at the Philadelphia mint in 1909, a century after the birth of Abraham Lincoln.

The eminent authority on Islamic coins, Stephen Album, states that the phrase "In God We Trust" is an English imprint of an Arabic phrase that was struck in Baghdad at the beginning of the ninth century AD.[4] The Arabic phrase, *lillah*, "for God" was widely distributed on the Abbasid Dynasty's coins following the initial striking by Caliph al-Ma'mun, son of al-Rashid (of One Thousand and One Nights fame). The Sufid coin displayed here came from a Muslim dynasty (AD 1361–1372) in the eastern Persian province of Khwarizm after the destruction of the Abbasid caliphate. Included in its unique boxed calligraphy are *lillah* and the divine names The King, The One, and The Victorious.

Fig. 95—Persian Coin Proclaims "for God"

---

4. Album, *Checklist of Islamic Coins*, 55.

Enshrined on the one cent US coin above President Lincoln's head is the phrase, "In God We Trust." This phrase was gradually added to all US coins beginning in the dark days of the Civil War. The Lincoln cent was minted in San Francisco in 1946. A copper two-cent piece, dated 1865, Philadelphia mint, and a Standing Liberty quarter, dated 1917, from the Denver mint, all proclaim, "In God We Trust."

Fig. 96—Three Coins "In God We Trust"

When western nations adopted Arabic numbers to replace the awkward Roman numerals and the equally cumbersome counting tables, the Europeans proceeded to accept a single unifying date. Previous dates on coins and official documents depended on birth, death, or enthronement of the individual rulers or other governing bodies. In the Palestinian port city of Acre an Arabic coin first exhibited a fixed date of 1251. The Christians' occupation of this city, strategic for the Western Crusaders, was about to end, but a sizeable Arab-Christian community still resided in Acre. These native Palestinians showed their allegiance to Jesus rather than a western king. They established the date of the coin: *year one thousand and two hundred and fifty one of the incarnation*. In the center of the dated text on this silver *dirham* is a cross. The reverse side (left) adds *the father, the son and holy spirit*. After years of rejecting the infidels' Arabic numbers and language by reigning Latin kings and popes, the BC/AD dates were set which confirmed the magi's study of an eclipse over Bethlehem's skies in April, 6 BC.

ANTIQUITY IN US COINS

Fig. 97—Silver Coin Date of Incarnation

Those anonymous Arabic Christians might not have survived as the Muslims under Mamluk Egyptian leaders claimed that they wiped out all of the Christians in Acre in their *Reconquista* of the Holy Land. The unintended consequences of this threat would be the discovery of America as Columbus sailed into the new world hoping to open the sea route to India. Further on, Columbus's successors turned their explorations into exploitation of the natives and an unfettered passion for gold. Other unintended consequences of this were the bankruptcy of Spain, the Inquisition, etc. This dark side of human history overshadowed what was going on at the street level where coins served as peaceful market transactions such as paying rent or a servant her wages. The dull domestic activities do not receive a fraction of the attention as the big guy on a coin's face, but the gold coins of caesars, shahs, and kings were spent, often recklessly, on wars and bribes for peace that lessened the values of the bronze *prutahs* needed for loaves of bread.

"In God We Trust" on US coins is a symbol of sacred and secular coexistence that ideally serve to unify a nation. Coins and paper currencies remind their holders to trust their government and to extend this trust to God. The previous pages supply images and texts that point out that the very minting process, the imprinting of figures and letters on coins during ancient Greek eras, was referred to as character, *Xaraktar* (Heb 3:1). Money represented the character of the government often certified by a human figure. Tiberius Caesar, as divine Augustus, was on the silver *drachm* coin that Jesus picked from the pocket of one of his detractors in the Temple episode recorded in three gospels (see Fig. 25).

Pictographic figures and renderings throughout this book are witnesses to the history of how kingdoms of antiquity and the three Abrahamic monotheistic faiths trusted in the character of their governing authorities and our Almighty Supreme Being. The written records combined with the archaeological findings are cautionary statements about abuses that defined legal and just weights of shekels as justice for the poor in the Hebrew Bible. In the gospel, Jesus asks us to observe with him the widow depositing her fractional mite in the Temple box and heed his warnings and judgments on those who fill up their moneybags on earth, forsaking any treasures in heaven (Luke 12:33). The issue of storage of excesses in bigger barns or hiding silver and gold in the ground was presented by an obscure Muslim leader (see Fig. 69) who stamped on an oversize silver coin the Qur'an's warning to Christian monks about burying coins and not spending in the "way of Allah" (Surah 9:34). Burying your gold has unintended consequences, as George Herbert, the seventeenth-century pastor poetically renders:

> Money, thou bane of bliss and source of woe,
> When coms't thou, that thou art so fresh and fine?
> I know thy parentage is base and low:
> Man found thee poor and dirty in a mine.
> Surely thou didst so little contribute
> To this great kingdom which thou now has got,
> That he was fain, when thou wert destitute,
> To dig thee out of thy dark cave and grot:
> Thus forcing thee, by fire he made thee bright:
> Nay, Thou have got the face of man; for we
> Have with our stamp and seal transferred our right:
> Thou art the man, and man but dross to thee.
> Man calleth thee his wealth, who made thee rich,
> And while he digs thee out, falls in the ditch.[5]

---

5. Herbert, "Money, Thou Bane of Bliss," 277.

Appendix A

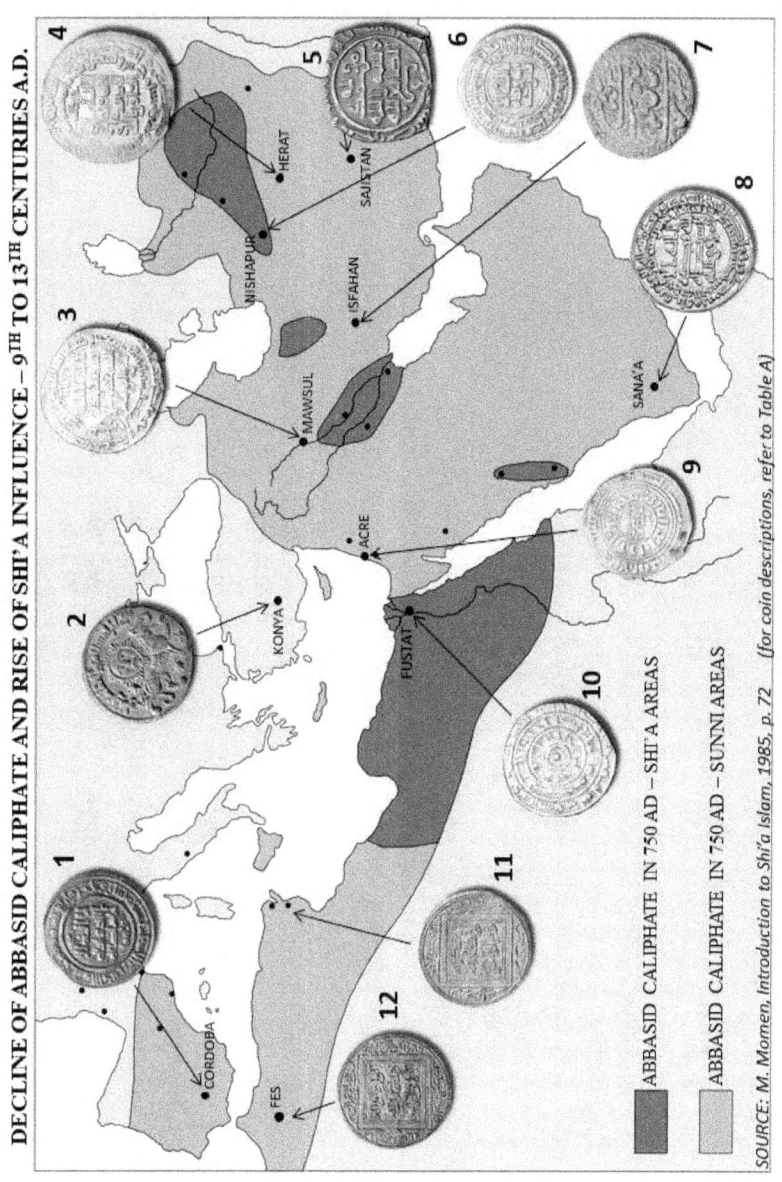

133

Table A

# on Map	Group	Denomination	Date (AH)	Ruler Date Range (AD)	Ruler named on coin	mint	metal	wt (g)	Reference (Album #)
1	'Abbadid of Sevilla	dinar	438	1042-1069	Al Mu'tadid 'Abbad	Sevilla	gold	3.24	A-402.1
2	Great Seljuk	dirham	640	1237-1246	Kai-Khusraw II	Qonya	silver	3.00	A-1218
3	Lu'lu'id (Zengid)	dinar	642	1234-1259	Badr al-Din Lu'lu'	al-Mawsil	gold	7.26	A-1871.4
4	Ghaznavid	dinar	395	998-1030	Mahmud	Herat	gold	3.26	A-1605
5	Saffarid	dinar	386	980-1003	Khalaf bin Ahmad (3rd)	Sajistan	gold	1.59	A-1420.1
6	Samanid	dinar	343	954-961	'Abdul Malik I bin Nuh	Nishapur	gold	4.33	A-1460
7	Safavid	ashrafi	1142	1723-1732	Shah Tahmasp	Isfahan	gold	3.48	A-2688
8	Abbasid-Yemen	dinar	272	870-892	Abu Al-'Abbas Ahmad al'Mu'tamid ala Allah	Sana'a	gold	2.93	A-1055
9	Crusader	bezant	(no date)	13th Cent.	al-Amir al-Mansur	Acre	gold	3.50	A-730
10	Fatimid	dinar	363	952-976	Ma'ad al Mu'izz	al-Kahirra	gold	3.76	A-697.1
11	Hafsids	dinar	(no date)	1230-1249	Abu Zakariah Yahya I	Sabta	gold	4.75	A-499.2
12	Merinid	dinar	(no date)	1244-1258	Abu Yahya Abu Bakr ibn Al-Haqq	(no mint cited)	gold	4.64	A-520

Appendix B

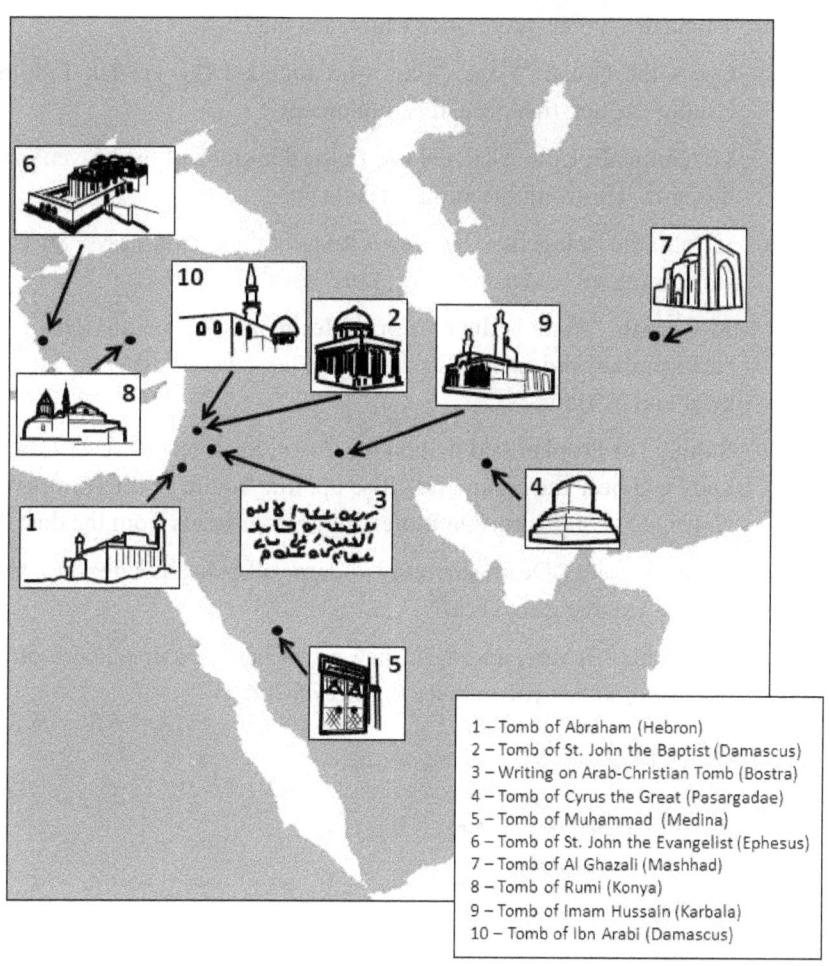

Table B

Tombs and Coins, Silent Sanctuaries of God's Eternity

Final words extracted from the final resting places of men of faith

1. Abraham: "I am a stranger and a sojourner among you; give me property among you for a burying place, that I may bury my dead out of my sight."[1]
2. St. John the Baptist: "He [Jesus] must increase, but I must decrease."[2]
3. 'Ulaih Christian Arab tombstone: "Allah pardon to 'Ulaih, son of 'Ubaidah . . . may have notice who reads this."[3]
4. Cyrus the Great: "I am Cyrus who founded the Persian Empire. Grudge me not, therefore, this monument."[4]
5. Muhammad: "Unto Allah belongeth the dominion of the heavens and the earth. He giveth life and He taketh."[5]
6. St. John the Evangelist: "He who testifies of these things says, 'Surely I am coming soon.' Amen. Come, Lord Jesus!"[6]
7. Al-Ghazali: "None is the creator of death and of life but God—may He be praised and exalted, so there is no life-giver or slayer but God—great and glorious."[7]
8. Rumi: "The Prophet said that on the Day of Resurrection, every single body will hear the command, 'Rise up.' The 'sound of the trumpet' is Holy God's command: 'Oh motes, lift up your heads from the dust.'"[8]
9. Imam Hussein: "Death surrounds Adam's offspring as a necklace surrounds a young girl's neck."[9]
10. Ibn Arabi: "Beware, and again beware, of being occupied with other than God, so that you may see the face of God."[10]

1. Gen 23:4 RSV.
2. John 3:30 RSV.
3. *Travels of Ali Bey, 19th Century.*
4. Cyrus tomb, Pasargadae.
5. Qur'an, 9:16.
6. John 3:30 RSV.
7. Al-Ghazali, *Ninety-nine Names of God*, 81.
8. Chittick, *Sufi Path of Love*, 102.
9. Ansary, *Destiny Disrupted*, 68.
10. Hirtenstein, *Unlimited Mercifier*, 209.

Bibliography

Album, Stephen. *Checklist of Islamic Coins*, 3rd edition. Santa Rosa, CA: Stephen Album Rare Coins, 2011.
Al-Ghazali, Abu Hamid. *The Ninety-nine Names of God*. Translated by David Burrell and Nazih Daher. Cambridge, UK: Islamic Texts, 1992.
Ali, Abdullah Yusuf. *The Meaning of the Holy Qur'an*. Beltsville, MD: Amana, 1989.
Ansary, Tamin. *Destiny Disrupted: A History of the World through Islamic Eyes*. New York: Public Affairs, 2009.
Arndt, William F., and F. Wilbur Gingrich. *A Greek-English Lexicon of the New Testament*. Chicago: University of Chicago Press, 1952.
Aziz, Joseph. *Priest and Prophet*. Translated by David Bentley. Los Angeles: Pen, 2005.
Barkay, Gabriel. "Riches of Ketef Hinnom." In *Biblical Archaeology* 200 (2009) 22–35.
Barnstone, Willis, and Marvin Meyer, eds. *The Gnostic Bible: Gnostic Texts of Mystical Wisdom from the Ancient and Medieval Worlds—Pagan, Jewish, Christian, Mandaean, Manichaean, Islamic, and Cathar*. Boston: New Seeds, 2006.
Bentley, David. *The 99 Beautiful Names*. 1999. Reprint, William Carey Library. Eugene, OR: Wipf & Stock, 2018.
Bergreen, Laurence. *Marco Polo: From Venice to Xanadu*. New York: Vintage, 2007.
Bowersock, G. W. *Roman Arabia*. Cambridge, MA: Harvard University Press, 1983.
Boyce, Mary, and Frantz Grenet. *A History of Zoroastrianism, Vol III*. 3 vols. Leiden: E. J. Brill, 1991.
Bright, John. *A History of Israel*. Philadelphia: Westminster, 1959.
Brock, Sebastian. *The Luminous Eye: The Spiritual World Vision of St. Ephrem*. Kalamazoo, MI: Cistercian, 1992.
Brown, Harold. *Heresies: Heresy and Orthodoxy in the History of the Church*. Peabody, MS: Hendrickson, 1984.
Cartledge, Paul. *Alexander the Great-The Hunt for a New Past*. Woodstock, NY: Overlook, 2004.
Cartwright, T. B. "Star of Bethlehem Coins—A Set of Serial Commemoratives." www.forumancientcoins.com/numiswiki/data/cartwright/Star%20of%20Bethlehem%20Coins.pdf.
Chittick, William C. *The Sufi Path of Love, the Spiritual Teachings of Rumi*. Albany: State University of New York, 1983.
Damascene, John. "Day of Resurrection." In *Methodist Hymnal*, translated by J. M. Neale, 151. New York: Methodist, 1939.

BIBLIOGRAPHY

Dionysius. *Pseudo-Dionysius: The Complete Works*. Translated by Colm Luibheid and Paul Rorem. New York: Paulist, 1987.
Eusebius. *The History of the Church from Christ to Constantine*. Translated by G. A. Williamson. New York University Press, 1966.
Feiler, Bruce. *Where God was Born—A Daring Adventure*. New York: Harper Perennial, 2005.
Feldman, Louis H. "Palestinian and Diaspora Judaism." In *Christianity and Rabbinic Judaism: A Parallel History of Their Origins and Early Development*, edited by Hershel Shanks, 1–39. Washington DC: Biblical Archaeology Society, 1992.
Ford, James. "Zoroaster & the Dawning of Monotheism." https://patheos.com/blogs/monkeymind/2014/03/zoroaster-the-dawning-of-monotheism.html.
Fowden, Garth. *Before and after Muhammad*. Princeton: Princeton University Press, 2004.
Goldziher, Ignaz. *Introduction to Islamic Theology and Law*. Translated by Andras and Ruth Hamori. Princeton: Princeton University Press, 1981.
Hendin, David. *Cultural Change: Jewish, Christian, Islamic Coins of the Holy Land*. New York: American Numismatic Society, 2011.
Hengel, Martin, and Anna M. Schwemer. *Paul between Damascus and Antioch*. Louisville: Westminster John Knox, 1997.
Herbert, George. "Money, Thou Bane of Bliss." In *Golden Treasury of Lyrical Poems*, edited by Oscar Williams, 277. New York: Mentor, 1953.
Hirtenstein, Stephen. *The Unlimited Mercifier: The Spiritual Life and Thought of Ibn 'Arabi*. Ashland, OR: Anqa, 1999.
Hock, Ronald F. *The Social Context of Paul's Ministry: Tentmaking and Apostleship*. Minneapolis: Fortress, 2007.
Hoeberichts, J. *Francis and Islam*. Quincy, IL: Franciscan, 1997.
Jenkins, Philip. *The Lost History of Christianity—The Thousand-year Golden Age*. New York: Harper Collins, 2008.
Joseph, John. *Nestorians and Muslim Neighbors*. Princeton: Princeton University Press, 1961.
Karabell, Zachary. *Peace be upon You: Fourteen Centuries of Muslim, Jewish, and Christian Conflict and Cooperation*. New York: Vintage, 2007.
King, Charles William. *The Gnostics and Their Remains: Ancient and Medieval*. New York: G. P. Putman's Sons, 1887.
Klimkeit, Hans-Joachim. *Gnosis on the Silk Road*. San Francisco: Harper San Francisco, 1993.
Lamb, Harold. *Genghis Khan: Emperor of All Men*. New York: Bantam, 1965.
Layton, Bentley. *The Gnostic Scriptures: A New Translation*. New York: Doubleday, 1987.
Lopez-Baralt, Luce. "St. John of the Cross and Ibn 'Arabi." In *Journal of Ibn 'Arabi Society*, edited by Stephen Hirtenstein, 76–78. Oxford: Ibn 'Arabi Society, 2000, 50–90.
Lossky, Vladimir. *The Mystical Theology of the Eastern Church*. Translated by the Fellowship of St. Albans and St. Sergius. Cambridge, UK: James Clark, 1998.
Louth, Andrew. *St. John Damascene: Tradition and Originality in Byzantine Theology*. Oxford: Oxford University Press, 2001.
Matheson, Sylvia. *Persia: An Archaeological Guide*. London: Trinity, 1972.
Molnar, Michael. *The Star of Bethlehem: The Legacy of the Magi*. New Brunswick, NJ: Rutgers University Press, 2013.
Momen, Moojan. *An Introduction to Shi'i Islam: The History and Doctrines of Twelver Shi'ism*. New Haven: Yale University Press, 1985.

Moulton, James. *The Treasure of the Magi: A Study of Modern Zoroastrianism*. London: Oxford University Press, 1917.
Murata, Sachiko. *The Tao of Islam. A Sourcebook on Gender Relationships in Islamic Thought*. Albany: State University of New York Press, 1992.
O'Conner, David, and Eric Clines, eds. *Amenhotep III: Perspectives on His Reign*. Ann Arbor: University of Michigan Press, 1998.
Pagels, Elaine. *Beyond Belief: The Secret Gospel of Thomas*. New York: Random House, 2003.
Pritchard, James, ed. *The Ancient Near East: An Anthology of Texts and Pictures*. Princeton: Princeton University, 1958.
Sanadiki, Khaled. *Legends & Narratives of Islam: The Biblical Personalities*. Chicago: Kazi, 2000.
Sayles, Wayne. *Ancient Coin Collecting, IV: Non-Classical Cultures*. Iola, WI: Krause, 1999.
Schaff, Philip. *History of the Christian Church, Vol III*. 7 vols. New York: Charles Scribner's Sons, 1914.
———. *History of the Christian Church, Vol IV*. 7 vols. New York: Charles Scribner's Sons, 1914.
———. *History of the Christian Church, Vol V*. 7 vols. New York: Charles Scribner's Sons, 1914.
Silberman, Neil Asher. *Heavenly Powers: Unraveling the Secret History of the Kabbalah*. Edison, NJ: Castle, 2000.
Spengler, William, and Wayne Sayles. *Turkoman Figural Bronze Coins. Vol I*. Lodi, WI: Clio's Cabinet, 1992.
———. *Turkoman Figural Bronze Coins. Vol II*. Lodi, WI: Clio's Cabinet, 1996.
Talman, Herbert Cushing. *A Guide to the Old Persian Inscriptions*. New York: American, 1893.
Tang, Li. *From the Oxus River to the Chinese Shores: Studies of East Syriac Christianity*. Wiesbaden, Germany: Orientalia Biblica et Christiana, 2011.
Thapar, Romila. *Aśoka and the Decline of the Mauryas*. New Delhi: Oxford Press India, 1997.
VanderKam, James C. *The Dead Sea Scrolls Today*. Grand Rapids: Eerdmans, 1993.
Wang, Helen. *Money on the Silk Road: The Evidence from Eastern Central Asia to c. AD 800*. London: British Museum Press, 2004.
Ward-Perkins, John, and Amanda Claridge. *Pompeii 79, Essay and Catalog*. New York: Alfred A. Knopf, 1978.
Winter, Bruce W. *Divine Honours for the Caesars: The First Christians' Responses*. Grand Rapids: Eerdmans, 2015.
Young, Edward J. *An Introduction to the Old Testament*. Grand Rapids: Eerdmans, 1960.

Index

99 Names of God, 94–95, 99–101

Abraham, vii, 13–14, 135–36
Abraxas, Gnostic God, 57–60, 109, 128
Acre, Palestinian seaport, 117, 122, 130–31
Alexander, the Great, 8, 21–22, 26, 59, 83, 116
Al-Ghazali, 94, 99–101, 135–36
Amenhotep IV (Akhenaten), 1–9, 80
amulet, see bulla
Antioch, 27–28, 47, 49–50, 126
Armenian, 77, 84, 117, 119
Aśoka, Emperor, 1, 7–11, 59, 81
Athena, goddess, 51–52, 125
Augustus, see Caesar Augustus

Baghdad, 99, 113, 119, 129
Bar Kochba Revolt, 36–37
Buddhism, 8, 107–8, 112
bulla, amulet, 41–42, 48
Byzantine Empire, 67, 69, 71, 84, 105, 110

Caesar Augustus, 29–30, 33, 49
    Claudius, 42
    Decius, 68–69, 90–92
    Diocletian, 69
    Julius, 33
    Nero, 55–56, 126
    Philip, 68–69
    Tiberius, Front cover, 33–34, 131
    Titus, 35–36

Caliph, David, 88–89
    Abd al-Malik, 76, 92–93, 97
    Harun al-Rashid 98, 129
    Al-Ma'mum, 105, 129

Damascus, 53, 67, 74–76, 103
Daniel, 20–23, 34–35, 80–81, 84, 89
David, 18–19, 25, 88–89
Darius, 82–83
Dead Sea Scrolls, 23–24, 60
Decius, see Caesar
Dome of the Rock, Jerusalem, 86, 96–97
Dionysius, Pseudo-Areopagite, 73–74, 102
drachma, denarius, coin, 40

Elijah, 19, 73, 94
Elohim, see YHWH (LORD)
Ephrem, the Syrian, 70–72, 95–96
Ephesus, 47–48

Francis of Assi, 119–20
Galatians, Paul's letter, 49–50, 53
Genghis Khan, 100, 117–19, 122
Gnosticism, 57–66, 72, 108–9
Gospel of Mathew, 27–28, 31–33, 61
    Mark, 38, 92
    Luke, 26, 30
    John, 31, 37–38

Herbert, George, 132
Heraclius, Emperor, 105, 110

INDEX

Ialdabaoth, Gnostic demigod, 64–65
Ibn Arabi, 119–21, 135–36
Ibn Taymiyah, 103–4
Ishmael, vii, 14, 53

Jehoash, Judean King, 19–20, 37
Jerusalem, see Temple
Jesus, life and kerygma, 25–35, 37–40, 66, 92, 108
John, the Baptist, 65, 135–36
John of Damascus, 74–77, 92, 105
John of the Cross, 120–21

Khusro, see Sasanian Emperor
Kublai Khan, 111, 119

Lady Liberty dime, see Tyche
Lincoln cent, 129

magi, magians, 27–29, 50, 82–84, 107, 110
Mani, Manichaeism, 63, 84, 107–110, 112
Mary, Jesus' mother, 26–28, 75, 97
Mecca and Medina, 87–88, 104
Melqarth, Tyrian shekel, coin, 40, 12–13, 17, 19, 23–24, 32–33, 35, 127
Moses, 12–16, 31–32, 42–43, 65, 80, 88–90
Molnar, Michael, astronomer, 27–29, 49–50
Muhammad, Prophet, 87–88, 93–94, 96, 104, 135–36

Nabatean, King Aretas IV, 53–54, 79
Nag Hammadi manuscripts, 60–66
Nero, see Caesar
Nestorian Christians, 70, 77–79, 108, 112–13, 116, 118
Nicene Creed, 70, 92

Parable of the Sower, Jesus, 92, Qur'an, 92, Gnostic, 61, Parthian, 108

Paul, Apostle, 30, 42–56, 73, 126
Parthian Empire, 28–29, 84, 108
Polo, Marco, 111–12, 119, 122
Pompeii, 48–49
Pontus Pilate, 47–48, 128–29
Priscilla and Aquila, tabernacle makers, 42, 44, 46–48
prutot, coin, 35, 39–40

Qur'an, 66, 88–92, 95, 97–98, 102, 104, 106, 120–21, 132

Richard the Lionhearted, 122
Romans, Paul's letter, 52–53
Rumi, poet theologian, 100–103

Saladin, 117, 122
Sasanian Emperor Shapur II, 84
　Khusro II, 85
　Queen Buran, 85
Sarah and Hagar, 14, 50
Septuagint Bible, 53, 57
Shekel, see Melqarth
Sleepers of the Cave, 90–92
Sunnah, Shi'a divisions, 99, 104, 133, 135–36

tabernacle makers, minters, see Priscilla, Aquila
Tabernacle, Wilderness tent, 16
Tetradrachm, coin, 40, 52
Temple, Jerusalem, 18–20, 22–23, 32–37
Tiberius, see Caesar
Tyche, goddess, 29, 50, 126

Wahabi, 103

YHWH (LORD), Names of God, Elohim, 12–15, 25

Zororoastrism, 21, 80–83, 101

www.ingramcontent.com/pod-product-compliance
Lightning Source LLC
Chambersburg PA
CBHW072143160426
43197CB00012B/2225